Willard

MEMOIRS OF THE
GATEKEEPER

MEMOIRS OF THE GATEKEEPER

THE TRUE STORIES BEHIND UNCOVERING SOME OF THE **BIGGEST SCANDALS** IN RECENT U.S. HISTORY

JOHN J. CRONIN, JR., CPA

AS TOLD TO WILLIAM FLEMING

Deeds Publishing | Athens

Published by Deeds Publishing in Athens, GA
www.deedspublishing.com

Printed in The United States of America

Cover design by Mark Babcock.

ISBN 978-1-950794-49-2

Books are available in quantity for promotional or premium use. For information, email info@deedspublishing.com.

First Edition, 2021

10 9 8 7 6 5 4 3 2 1

To that small percentage of government employees without whose misdeeds this book and my career would not have been possible.

—*JJC, Jr.*

Contents

Introduction   ix

1. Watergate Rumblings   1
2. The Beginning   29
3. My First Audit — A Look At Congressional Perks   37
4. The Federal Meat Inspection Scandal — # B163450   43
5. The Banking Industry's Great Treasury Raid Of The 60'S   51
6. The National Park System — The Taxpayer Loses Again   61
7. Feeding At The Federal Grant Trough — Or —
   How Not To Play Politics — # B174895   69
8. An Early Look At The CIA   81
9. Auditing And Investigating The President
   Of The United States — # B133209   85
10. Some Things Never Die — Nixon
    White House Audit — # B133209   91
11. Audit Of Presidents' Unvouchered Accounts — # B133209   101
12. The Treasury Department Mistreats
    Our Nation's Heros — # B179225   115
13. The Federal Housing Scandals   129
    # FGMSD 77-33, # FGMSD 79-14, # FGMSD 80-43

14. HUD Disasters Continue   135
     # FGMSD 77-12, # FGMSD 79-41
15. The First GAO Sting Operation   151
     # FGMSD 80-65
16. The Energy Scandal — GAO/OCG – 82-1   159
17. The Investigation Of The CPA Profession   173
18. "Marcosgate"— The Investigation Of
     Ferdinand And Imelda Marcos — GAO/AFMD – 86-33   187
19. "Irangate"— Inside Iran-Contra   209
21. "Irangate"— The Conclusion   231
22. Issues With The Central Intelligence Agency   251
23. Was It Worth It?   255

About the Author   261

Introduction

Most of us are familiar with the political, governmental, and even criminal scandals that plagued America in the second half of the twentieth century—Watergate, Irangate, Marcosgate, and others. However, what is not widely known is the role that the Government's General Accounting Office played in investigating and exposing the frauds. One particular individual was a hard-nosed Irish CPA by the name of John Cronin—or as he came to be known—the Gatekeeper.

The General Accounting Office (GAO), now known as the Government Accountability Office, was created by Congress in 1921. It is the auditing and investigative arm of the Congress. It is headed by the U.S. Comptroller General, an appointed position, renewable every fifteen years.

Its initial focus was to review the propriety of the hundreds of thousands of paper vouchers sent annually to the Government in Washington, D.C. for reimbursement. They were usually wrapped in red cloth for shipping—hence the term "government red tape".

By the end of World War II, the GAO had 14,000 employees, but automation and the transfer of some functions to other agencies quickly reduced the force to about 5,000 by 1950. In that year, Congress passed the Accounting and Auditing Act which greatly expanded the GAO's authority to conduct audits and financial reviews at the Executive Branch. In 1954, President Eisenhower appointed Joseph Campbell as Comptroller General—the first to be a Certified Public Accountant (CPA). Campbell immediately began a recruitment program of college graduate accountants and stressed they earn their CPA degree.

Cronin began his GAO career in 1956 and served in an ever-expanding watchdog capacity for thirty-three tumultuous years under six different Presidents. Reader beware, many of his investigations and assignments described herein necessarily had overlapping timelines. This book is a personal chronicle of his most notorious GAO investigations—directly as he witnessed them from the trenches.

He led investigations and audits of Watergate, Marcosgate, Irangate, and many others—earning him the nickname "the Gatekeeper." His activities clearly dispense with the myth that accountants lead dull and boring lives.

Following many chapters there is a GAO Report number. Should the reader want to examine and research the full report of an investigation, please go to www.GAO.gov and enter the number.

1. Watergate Rumblings

After sixteen years as an auditor/investigator for the General Accounting Office, I guess some of the glamour and excitement of the position had begun to wear off. Sure, there had been a few complex investigations, but mostly pretty mundane stuff—if you consider government waste mundane. But I liked it that way. Just take the assignment, follow the audit program and required audit standards, help process and issue the report. Saving the government money was straightforward, satisfying work. There were only two things I didn't particularly like. The first was that every few years a new president with a new agenda and team of hotshot politicos would take over; the second was the Washington D.C. summer heat.

At the time, all federal agencies were required to provide space for GAO operations within their headquarters building. In many cases however, these audit sites ended up nearby in rented commercial space. These facilities were frequently sub-standard because the GAO was certainly not most agencies best friend. At the moment I had set up on the second floor of a narrow building above a Chinese restaurant on G Street. It took a while to get used to the smell of the cooking, but at least it was only half a block from the main Treasury Department building—the initial focus of my investigation into the Watergate mess.

It was a typical beastly-hot mid-August day in Washington in 1972, so my mood wasn't great to begin with. Although I was in my "new" office on "G" Street, the cooking odor was bad and the air conditioning was marginal. I hardly noticed. I was too busy at my desk trying to deal with the aftermath of a major reorganization involving my department. Often there is a good and bad side to a restructuring; the good side was that I was assigned to a new position. It certainly sounded interesting. I was now responsible for conducting reviews and investigations of accounting systems and related financial issues at all the civil agencies of the federal government. This meant that at age thirty-eight I was in position to be an Assistant Director of the independent audit and investigating arm of the Congress—the United States General Accounting Office.

What then, could be the down side? I had only to look around me. I now knew why my transfer to this newly created division—Financial & General Management Studies Division (FGMSD) had taken so long. The position was offered to me by the new GAO Director, Don Scantlebury, but most of the staff had been involuntarily transferred, due no doubt to the unknown nature of its entire mission. I had heard a rumor that the pre-existing line divisions were making last minute substitutions to the names to be transferred. They were placing their poor and borderline performers in the jobs and functions scheduled to be transferred—not an uncommon trick in both government and industry.

My personal share of this disaster was two staff members with drinking problems, one with emotional disorders and all with average or worse performance ratings. The two with drinking problems were to be my senior managers, reporting directly to me. One of them had been my boss ten years earlier and was responsible for one of my early promotions. On the positive side I also had four capable staffers at the operating level who had volunteered to join the new division. However, their early training caused them to prefer financial analysis work rather than evaluating the effectiveness of federal programs — exactly what now was being stressed to be our primary mission by the current Comptroller General, Elmer Staats.

So there I was with a second-rate team and lousy air conditioning, trying to get a handle on assignments already in progress. Then of course there was our primary responsibility — to develop a detailed work plan for operating accounting systems in agencies for the new division. The plan was to establish financial review protocols in most of the major federal civil agencies — an enormous undertaking. Since GAO reports to Congress, there exists an Office of Congressional Relations (OCR). Many Representatives and Senators ask the GAO for help with personal concerns or committee matters via the OCR. The OCR determines if the issue in within GAO jurisdiction or is more of a constituent concern. If a committee Chair makes the request, GAO is required by law to act.

The phone ringing jolted my concentration and my secretary announced a call from Marty Fitzgerald, the Director of the GAO Office of Congressional Relations. I couldn't tell from his voice if he was being serious but Marty congratulated me on my new position. He advised that his office had received a request from a member of Congressman Phil Burton's staff. They wanted a briefing by the GAO on the set up of the White House payroll system and how it worked. Since the White House was considered a civil agency, the request was assigned to me.

Each year GAO routinely handles several thousand requests

from members of Congress and their staffs. As such, I did not consider anything unusual, nor did Marty. He told me to contact a Mr. Gary Sellers, a staff member to Congressman Burton.

Congress was in summer recess and things in Washington were pretty quiet. By now most of the media hoopla seemed to have died down over the Watergate break-in at Democratic Campaign Headquarters, a whole four weeks earlier. Most people considered the event a dumb political act. A clumsy operation by some over-zealous political types tied to some consultant that occasionally worked at the White House. After all, in August of 1972 President Nixon was considered a shoe-in for a second term. Everybody was thinking about the heat and vacations but not necessarily in that order. My plans to take my wife Lorraine and the kids to Maine for a week of course were immediately tabled by the new assignment.

I called Sellers and arranged for a meeting. He wanted to see me right away and oddly, declined any details of what he wanted, other than an explanation of how the White House accounting system worked. I was able to put off the meeting until the next day, August 14. In the meantime, I researched and found out that several years earlier the GAO had helped the White House design their accounting system. I got a copy of the manual and reviewed it. Their system was rather basic. The General Services Administration preparing the payroll and other expenditures and sending it to the Treasury Department to process the vouchers for payment. This was a fairly standard practice, largely manual, that ironically would later become a great help to us.

The next morning I took staff member Dave Yeakel with me and we headed for Congressman Burton's office on Capitol Hill. I identified myself to one of the Congressman's secretaries and moments later Gary Sellers appeared from a nearby room and introduced himself. He was a short man with a moustache and a somewhat unkempt look—and a fast talker. He advised that our meeting would be in another office, so we followed him to another part of the Longworth House Office Building where we entered the offices not of Congressman Burton, but those of Congressman Les Aspin. The secretary seemed to know Sellers well and told us to go right in—"they" were waiting.

There sat Congressman Aspin and his Administrative Assistant Bill Broderick—it was beginning to look like we had been sandbagged.

Alongside the Congressman sat a huge white shaggy dog that stared at me as if I were his next meal. That might actually have been preferable treatment than what I expected from the notorious Congressman.

Aspin started the meeting by stating he had serious concerns that the President of the United States and several of his aids had committed dangerous violations of criminal law. He wanted the GAO to investigate the matter. I started to break out in a cold sweat.

This could cost me my promotion.

The meeting then was turned over to Sellers and Broderick to get into the dirty details and they did the rest of the talking. First they made a series of general allegations about a group of cutthroats they called "the plumbers." There were included references to the Watergate break-in which they alleged was planned by the President.

"Nixon thinks he's king, above the law," said Sellers.

"Yes, King Richard, he does whatever he wants," echoed Broderick.

I tried to speak up, saying that was preposterous but was cut off. The term "vendetta" crossed my mind.

On several occasions they said he had ceased to be a legitimate President. Another thing that worried me was they said they were working with a little known congressional "organization" known as the Democratic Study Group. I had heard of it but knew few details other than that they and the Republican counterpart studied partisan political issues that were not the focus of the regular public congressional committee structure.

One has to understand that normally at a meeting between a member of Congress and the GAO, one of our OCR liaisons and an Assistant Director or higher would be present. They would handle any sensitive issues and negotiate major commitments for us. With no help in sight, I knew I was on my own—and I didn't like the smell of this setup at all. I knew the standard GAO policy on not investigating anything before the courts, such as Watergate or anything involving criminal wrongdoing. But then Aspin had to have known this too…but on they ranted.

Talk about trial by fire on the first day of a new job.

Trying to hide my sweaty hands and buy a little time, I took a deep breath. I very nervously but precisely stated our formal, statutory policy. That did not slow them down for a second, since as I had guessed, they did know our policy and the law.

"Don't bother to quote me the law," roared Aspin, "just get in there and find out what the hell is going on!"

Beyond just sweaty palms, now my heart was racing.

Sellers continued to do most of the talking which at times could be better classified as a tirade. At one point Broderick broke in, "Oh Mr. Cronin, you don't understand. We don't want you to investigate Watergate and the criminal activity of Nixon and his cronies. We just want you to examine all payroll transactions and vouchers for the last two years to assure they are legal, valid, and correct. I believe that is in one of GAO's basic legislative mandates in the 1921 law that created your organization. I believe it is referred to as your responsibility to audit and settle the accounts of the accountable officers of the government and I believe the administrative officer at the White House is one of those officers."

Well, there you have it. With that little prepared speech, it was clear they had done their homework. To use some football jargon, it was time to fade back 10 and punt. Eying the door in hopes of a quick escape, I referred to the papers on the White House accounting system I had brought with me and summarized how its payroll and voucher system worked.

The meeting was already difficult enough when the Congressman's large dog with the hungry eyes strolled across the room and put his head on my lap. Friendly so far, I thought. But he began to drool all over my papers and notes for what seemed like an eternity, but it was only a few seconds until one of the staff dragged him off to a corner and told him to be still. While to this day I'm not sure he had been given the "drool command", I got the distinct impression that the dog had participated in many congressional meetings.

When I finished my by-the-book-briefing on the accounting system, I advised the Congressman that I was not in a position to make a commitment to do the work they had requested. I promised to discuss the matter with the Comptroller General and get back to them as soon as I could. Aspin ended the meeting by rehashing what Sellers and Broderick had said. "Tell the Comptroller General that I'm not about to let GAO off the hook on this one." I feared to speculate on what he meant by that. I guess he wanted to be sure I knew the severity of his orders.

Very little was said during the taxi ride back to my office. My nervousness had subsided somewhat but there were a thousand thoughts spinning in my head.

Isn't this a criminal matter?
Why the games around Aspin's involvement?
Was Nixon himself involved?
Why me — what did I do to deserve this?
I wish I was sailing with the family up in Maine.

Still in the cab, Dave asked, "John, what the hell are you going to do now?"

I sarcastically responded, "Well, I think I'll throw up except I'm not sure if it will be before or after I write the official Contact Memo." A Congressional Contact Memo is required to be sent to the OCR liaison office within 24 hours after any meeting with congressional staff.

"Just go by the book, John, go by the book."

As I dictated the Memo, I could see my promotion to Assistant Director disappearing. I had been caught in the middle of a very unpleasant and possibly spiteful situation. The GAO was and is a very conservative organization. It frowns on any staff getting the Office involved in political issues. This situation was certainly politically driven, not to mention the possible criminal aspects.

My memo was only two pages long. I had it hand carried to the OCR with a copy to my Division Director, Don Scantlebury. According to procedure, other carbon copies were locked in my safe. I finished the day unable to concentrate on other work, so I headed home.

In those days, Alexandria, Virginia was a very small, quiet, family- oriented community. We lived in a new two-bedroom garden apartment, off King Street. It was very adequate for my mid-level functionary taste, with a small balcony overlooking a tiny park. My wife Lorraine was seven months pregnant with our second child. When I walked through the door, she immediately sensed something was wrong.

"This has not been a good day."

"Oh really, I thought you'd be all bubbly over the new position. I made your favorite, stuffed pork chops for dinner—and here's your martini."

"I've been ordered to open an investigation of the President, and the Comptroller General is not happy."

I related to her the story of the day's activities. Knowing her concern over whether this would affect my career, I left out most of the unpleasant details and declared this to be a two martini night. Sleep came only intermittently as I knew I was in for a tough next day.

Like most mornings, I got to the office between 7:30 and 8:00 to beat the rush hour traffic and get through some paperwork before the phones started ringing. My sense of foreboding unfortunately was correct. It didn't take long for the Contact Memo to stir things up. At about 9:30 Marty Fitzgerald, our Director of Congressional Relations called and told me to get to the Comptroller General's private office immediately. They would wait for me outside the office until I caught a taxicab over. It is not very often that Audit Managers get summoned to the Comptroller General's office, or for that matter, even Assistant Directors. Most meetings at that level were with Division Directors or their Deputies and staff. The 10 blocks did not take long, but it was long enough for the nerves to begin to kick in again.

Maybe I should have been more upfront with Lorraine about the possible career risks of this assignment.

I walked up the stone steps with considerable trepidation. Then up to the seventh floor and down the immaculately polished hall. The walls were covered with what looked like black and white photographs of past Comptroller Generals—all seemingly glaring down at me.

"Go right in, they are waiting for you," said the prim, over-starched young executive assistant.

And waiting they were. Comptroller General Elmer Staats sat at the end of an en suite twenty-person mahogany conference table. The floors were covered with elegant oriental rugs and the walls with fine art. The set up placed the Deputy Comptroller General Bob Keller sitting on Staats' right with the entire five man congressional liaison staff running down the left. At the opposite end of the table was a solitary leather high-backed chair for me. It kind of looked like an electric chair.

Keller was a career GAO employee who rose through the ranks, a decent guy, very personable and well liked individual. With a broad smile he said, "Well John we saved the hot seat for you." While the others laughed since it was supposed to be funny, I gave him a nod and a grin which was about all I could do with the sudden unfunny knot in my stomach. With all this brass, this was clearly a very high-level meeting—and I was the "guest" of honor.

Staats took over the meeting and directly asked me what this was all about. He of course had read the Contact Memo but wanted the "between the lines" stuff. I related all the details of the meeting, including some of the heated exchanges and colorful language.

I did not include my personal thoughts, particularly as to Aspin's real motivation—completely political—was to discredit the President.

A discussion then followed where each man—in order of rank—carefully expressed their concern over our going into the White House to do such an audit. There were two primary reasons stated: one reason I had already given about not investigating criminal matters (which would change by statute ten years later) or matters before the courts. The second and more serious concern was that the GAO had stoically maintained its independence from politics since its inception in 1921. The type of work requested here could give the appearance that we were being used as a tool of one political party against the other.

Oh boy, here we go.

After about 30 minutes of further discussion, or rather posturing by the junior staff, a tactically safe way out was seemingly identified. Although as a matter of policy the GAO entertained legitimate requests from all members of Congress, our basic legislative mandate from the Budget and Accounting Act of 1921 only required us to undertake requests signed by one of the Chairmen of the standing committees of the Congress. It was decided that I was to take that message back to the Hill and tell Congressmen Aspin and Burton that since they were not Chairmen of standing committees, we would not be able to do the requested audit work.

I did not think too much of the idea because in the past we had done request work for both members. Futhermore, the "rule" was insane because we routinely ignored it and frequently processed requests from any congressman so long as they were within our jurisdiction. Nevertheless, I had my orders.

Cats ready to pounce, Broderick and Sellers were awaiting my call and set up a meeting with me within the hour. I explained we could not do the work they had requested because the members were not chairmen of standing committees. To use a popular expression "the shit hit the fan"—Broderick attacked first.

"Did you arrive at that position on your own? At what level in GAO was the decision made?"

"At the highest level."

"Do you mean the Comptroller General?" he snapped. I nodded yes.

Sellers then asked a rather odd question.

"Does it make any difference which standing committee chairman signs the request?"

When I said no, they asked if I could wait for a while which I did and they left the room. Thirty minutes later they returned with a letter signed by Pennsylvania Congressman John Dent, Chairman of Education and Labor, one of the standing committees. The letter asked for an audit of the White House. Handing me the letter, Sellers sneered, "Now see if you can get out of this one."

Returning from the Hill, I took the letter back to Marty Fitzgerald who read it but told me they had concocted a fallback plan.

...and what a plan it turned out to be.

I was told to contact the White House and tell them about the request as a test to see if they would try to claim executive privilege or use other political tactics to try to keep us out.

Back in my office and more concerned than ever, I called Wilbur Jenkins, the White House Administrative Officer. He was one of those expediter types we would call when we were about to start an audit or investigation. I explained that I was heading up the team at the GAO to audit the administrative expenses at the White House for the past several years which had been duly requested by Congress. I did not give any of the details. Also, I did not identify any of the individual congressional requesters, which was our policy, unless specifically authorized. Jenkins was business-like and even somewhat pleasant during the conversation.

He had had many dealings with GAO over the years and was quite familiar with our audit authority as contained in the original Act of 1921 that created GAO. He knew it gave us broad authority to access all Government books, documents, papers, and records.

The only thing he expressed some concern over was that this was a Congressional request and not a self-initiated GAO review. I think he may have sensed trouble. He promised to get back to me. Stomach again churning, I replaced the receiver.

The next day I received a call from a Noble Melencamp who introduced himself as the Executive Assistant to President Nixon. As I expected, he started to question me about the purpose and scope of the audit as well as our authority to conduct the investigation.

"I'm a little disturbed by your request and I doubt you have authority to examine presidential records."

"You know very well we do indeed have the authority," I replied with considerably more confidence than I expected.

I went on to outline the general scope of the audit and identified the requester as a congressional committee chairman but did not give him the name.

"Mr. Cronin, I want you to know it seems to me the GAO is playing politics with this." He was being forceful but polite and said someone would get back to me. Thus ended the first encounter with Melencamp.

The next day, White House Administrative Officer Jenkins called back and said we could come over and start the project. This was much to my surprise because I didn't expect the White House to roll over so easily. Personally, I felt the whole thing was a bit of a wild goose chase. I'd rather be using my new position working on the requests already sitting on my desk. I told him we would be over in the morning. I let the Comptroller General know and then advised Gary Sellers that we would be starting the next day.

Gary now finally went into the details and informed me they

wanted copies of payrolls for numerous specified periods. He needed a specific analysis of all consultant payments and detailed schedules for all travel and other administrative expense. The reference to the consultant payments made it clear to me that one of the things they were zeroing in on was the group that the nation would soon come to know as the "plumbers."

That night, another two martini dinner did not make sleeping any easier. I lay awake thinking about the next day, the enormity of the undertaking and the no-win situation I was in. I was being pulled three ways, by the Congress, the White House, and by an increasingly uneasy Comptroller General.

After what felt like two hours of sleep, morning eventually arrived. Despite the horrid Arlington traffic, I was at the office before 8AM for a planning session on the new request. I was determined to keep a "business as usual" low profile for the duration of the assignment. It was agreed that Dave Yeakle would lead the work, assisted by a junior staff member. We discussed how to handle the project and which physical records to request. We also talked about how and when we would keep Sellers and Broderick informed—as they requested, doled out piecemeal, or follow normal GAO procedure and issue a complete report.

Soon it was time for our first joint meeting which had been scheduled for 9am. Fortunately it was only a short three-block walk to the Old Executive Office building. It is a majestic building, high ceilings, ornate paneling, and with most of the rooms having marble fireplaces which were actually used for heating at the turn of the century. The three of us approached the uniformed Secret Service officers at the front desk, presented our credentials, and were told to wait. About ten minutes went by. A clerk showed up and we were buzzed through a locked gate and escorted to Room One, the White House Administrative Office. There

Wilbur Jenkins and his assistants Art Pettipas and Dick White were waiting, seated ominously at a huge antique conference table.

I had been at many audits in the preceding fifteen years but I sensed something here was different. Seated before us were three obviously nervous people. No one is overjoyed at a first meeting with auditors, particularly at the beginning of an audit of this size, scope, and sensitivity—but I certainly did not expect that from White House staff.

Why were they the nervous ones?

We explained the general nature of the Congressional request and that we wanted to see all payroll and other records, including those of all White House consultants. The mention of consultants seemed to get Jenkins even more upset as his hands visibly began to shake. In a somewhat lecturing tone, he explained that many expenditures, including consultants, were paid from an account called "Special Projects." That account was exempt from GAO audit and furthermore even within the regular accounts the President had the authority to certify selected payments as exempt from GAO review.

I always felt this was a rather direct undermining of the GAO mandate, but Jenkins was essentially correct. We were aware of the account and the President's special authority for the other accounts. However, we got a very fuzzy explanation of how and when the special authority could be used.

A phone rang at that point and Jenkins excused himself to take the call. When he returned he told me that Melencamp, the Executive Assistant to the President, wanted to talk just to the two of us.

I left my staff to begin work on the remaining procedural details and to set up a place to work. Jenkins and I headed for the

West Wing of the White House, where I had never been. Entering for the first time can be awesome and intimidating. White House officials often use the set up for just that purpose. We entered through a side door in the basement and Jenkins cleared me through the uniformed Secret Service officer. Several agents gave me the once-over.

So this is what it feels like to be x-rayed.

There was no doubt I was in the White House between the hovering Secret Service troops and the official trappings including beautiful large framed color photographs of the President and Mrs. Nixon at recent events. We entered an office off the lobby and I was introduced to Noble Melancamp, the Executive Assistant to the President. Melancamp was short compared to my 6'2" but somehow, I felt small. He was very formally dressed in a black suit and a black and white striped tie. He got right to the point, starting the conversation in a stern tone questioning our authority as well as our motives.

No big surprise there.

After once again explaining our authority and that the audit was in response to a Congressional request, Melancamp asked for the name of the requestor, even though I'm sure he knew the statutes. Citing our policy, I did not identify the requester.

"We'll just have to see about that later," he snapped.

Although upset, Melancamp to my surprise agreed to cooperate. This was likely because his ace in the hole was that historically the President has often used the principle of executive privilege in order to deny access to White House records.

Game on.

Then it was back to Jenkin's office to finalize the details of the audit. This part was not complicated, having done it countless times. We were given a small office near the administrative office and arrangements were made to put Dave, myself, and a junior staff member on the "access list." The access list is maintained by the uniformed Secret Service to admit individuals to the White House complex unescorted. Once this and a few other mundane mechanics were settled, I phoned the Comptroller General and Gary Sellers and let them know that we were in business.

We began by getting the payroll, travel, and related records for the preceding two years and started reviewing them. It was an awful lot of paper and we had no idea of the particular sums involved, so we initially concentrated on payments to consultants. We also asked for all records pertaining to Hunt, McGruder, McCord, Odle, Segretti, and Sloan. It didn't take long for some other of the now historic names to appear, such as Gordon Liddy and Howard Hunt.

The best we could determine immediately was that none of the "plumbers" were on the payroll on the day of the Watergate break-in. We made copies of many of the related payment documents. I made notes that many of the normal expenditure controls appeared to be missing or were incomplete. I noticed that a number of the payroll documents were signed by another Watergate figure, Jeb Magruder — the problem was, we had three distinct versions of his signature.

We knew there are often instances where the person signing has oral authorization to do so. Although technically illegal, and we have the authority to pursue, this abuse is rarely prosecuted. That of course does not make it legal, but if we put everybody in jail that signed someone else's name, there would be no room for the real criminals.

During this period, Sellers was getting increasingly difficult to deal with. Without explanation, he was asking for schedule after schedule and document after document. Suddenly we were not auditors but "gophers"—worse, I had no idea at the time where this was all going. Then several new problems developed.

We had asked the White House for supporting documentation for a number of specific payments. We were told these items had been certified by the President and were not available for review. After a hurried call to a GAO lawyer, I was told that they indeed did have that authority but there should be an actual certificate for the list, and I should ask for it. When I passed this information on to Jenkins, things began to deteriorate further.

I was told I had to meet with a lawyer by the name of Darlene Moulds who worked for John Dean. Meet we did, but nothing was accomplished because there was no official certificate. Jenkins and his staff had merely used a rubber stamp on the payment documents that read "by direction of the President." Ms. Moulds said she felt that was sufficient. During our meeting, which only lasted about 20 minutes, I noticed one of the doors to her office was ajar and I had the strange feeling we were not alone. I was right. As I got up to leave I glanced through the slightly open door and much to my amazement I saw that White House Counsel, John Dean, had been eavesdropping on our conversation.

It was clear that by going down this path we were getting nowhere on gaining true access to the payments in question. As an experienced GAO auditor with a specific, properly authorized mandate, being stonewalled like this was like waving a huge red flag in front of a charging bull. It only increased my resolve to find out what was really going on.

But obviously they were still at least one step ahead of us—but not for long. My junior auditor was a young, bright, relatively new employee. A self-starter, he was eager to impress his superiors with his observation skills as an auditor/investigator. While working through a pile of documents from his assigned desk in the

Administrative Offices, he noticed many White House staff members coming and going with what appeared to be large amounts of cash and checks. Lots of money was evidently changing hands. Without any consultation with Dave or me, he announced to Jenkins that he was going to do a surprise cash count of the money in his office safe.

I was back in my G street office when my secretary announced I had a call from Melancamp. I picked up the phone and never finished hello.

"Your damn smart-ass of an auditor just tried to access Jenkins' safe and count the cash. Those are not government funds, they are private funds available to the President and GAO has no business going anywhere near them. You get over here right now and call off the little son-of-a-bitch. If you don't I will personally throw every one of you out of the White House."

Now isn't this an interesting development?

I told him I personally would be right over since it was clear he was too hot under the collar to be reasoned with over the phone. When I walked into the room, I couldn't tell who was more upset, my staff or Jenkins' people. Since there was no record of the existence of a government cashier fund, I made a decision and informed Jenkins and his people that there would be no cash count—everybody calmed down.

Later, when I discussed it in private with my staff member, he told me he had seen several White House staff members cashing what appeared to be pay checks and overheard conversations. Apparently, they had received less cash than the amount of the check and several were not too happy. Also, there seemed to be an endless supply of cash.

Ok—Why the large stash of cash—and what was it being used for?

For the next couple of weeks, I was having regular meetings with Broderick and Sellers, supplying them with copies of the various schedules and documents we had gathered. They lit up like a Christmas tree when I told them about the safe and the "certified" payments. By now it was about the third week in September and most of Washington was concentrating on the election.

The next Friday, September 22, when we arrived at the White House we received a strange message from the Secret Service officer that had been admitting us every morning. He told us to make sure when we left that day we took all our belongings with us as we had been removed from the access list and would not be admitted the following Monday. No doubt the issues over the safe and the certified payments had triggered the action by John Dean.

Maybe we were getting a little too close…

Back at the office the reaction at GAO was one of relief. The Comptroller General, being a strictly by the numbers guy, did not want GAO involved in a political mess, much less having us act as "gophers" rather than auditors.

To put it mildly however, Sellers was not at all relieved — and now it was his turn to explode over the phone.

"King Richard can't just ignore Congress like that! We have a properly executed mandate. I'm going to take care of this."

That sounded to me like an idle threat since most of the Congressmen were out campaigning, but it turned out was I wrong. The weekend blissfully was quiet for a change as my wife Lorraine and I awaited the birth of our second child which would come just a week later.

Monday morning arrived and I tried to get back to managing my still fledgling organization. In my mind I considered (perhaps wishfully) the White House audit finished, and it was time to get on to other projects. There was one particularly difficult problem that required my immediate attention. An inherited staff member who years earlier had been my boss had developed a serious drinking and absentee problem. Following protocol, I immediately consulted with our GAO counselor. He was hired in response to recent legislation that required each agency to set up a program for substance abuse.

Harold, as we will call him, had not phoned in his last absence as required—he was too drunk. This gave me a chance to act. I refused to certify his payroll form as being "on duty" status and cut off his checks. This shook up our administrative section because no one had done this before—but this was serious and it stuck. All the professional counselors will tell you if you want to help an alcoholic you have to threaten their livelihood. In most cases paychecks were sent by mail to the employee's bank, so I called Harold to tell him what I had done. His wife said he was too drunk to come to the phone. It was 9:00 AM. She cried and said she needed money for food. But following the advice of the counselor I told her to get Harold to work. More about Harold later.

Just then one of my staff ran into the office asking if I had seen the Washington Post, which I had not. There it was—the headline said "NIXON EJECTS AUDITORS FROM WHITE HOUSE." The article referred to a press release by Congressman Les Aspin and openly accused the President of trying to hide wrongdoing from the GAO auditors by throwing them out. While it was traditional to blame something on the head man to get attention, at the time none of us had any idea how accurate that guess was. I originally attributed the backfired decision to end the audit to Dean and Melancamp who were no doubt trying to protect Nixon just before the election.

The fact that President Nixon was involved in the decision would not become known for two years. That was when Alexander

Butterfield made his famous disclosure about the secret tapes of oval office meetings. According to the tapes at 5:30 PM on September 15, 1972, the following conversation took place between the President, White House Council John Dean, and Chief of Staff Bob Haldeman.

DEAN: "And they're looking, this GAO audit that's going on right now, uh, I think that they have got some suspicion, uh, in even a cursory investigation, which is not going to discover anything, that they're going to find something here. I learned today incidentally, that, that, uh, I haven't confirmed this because it's—came from the GO, GAO auditor, investigator who's down here, that he is down here at the Speaker of the House's request, which surprised me.

Haldeman: Well, damn the Speaker of the House. Maybe we better put a little heat on him.

President: I think so too.

Haldeman: Because he's got a lot worse problems than he's going to find down here.

Dean: That's right.

Haldeman: That's the kind of thing –

President: I know, let the police department go.

Haldeman: That's the kind of thing that, you know, you—What we really ought to do is call the Speaker and say, "I regret to see you ordering GAO down here because of what it's going to cause us to require to do to you."

President: Why don't you just have Harlow go see him and tell him that?

Haldeman: Because he wouldn't do it.

President: Hmm?

Haldeman: 'Cause he wouldn't do it.

President: Harlow wouldn't do it, you mean.

Haldeman: Harlow would say, "Mr. Speaker—"
President: Yeah."

It would be two years before the Nixon tapes would be discovered and released and we would know the full truth. At this point however we had no choice but to try to return to the White House and reason with them to allow the audit.

We would be in for a surprise.

Back at my office the next day, it didn't take long for the phone to begin ringing. Maybe I'm superstitious, but I could swear calls coming from the White House rang with an ominous tone. At about 10:00, Noble Melencamp was on the phone. He was very apologetic and explained that there had been a terrible misunderstanding by the Secret Service and our access was cancelled in error. We didn't believe it. At that point I thought John Dean did it on his own, figuring he had had about enough of us.

We arranged a meeting with Wilbur Jenkins and his assistants Art Pettipas and Dick White. They had terrible bags under their bloodshot eyes and looked like they had been on a week-long drunk. Without having to ask, they handed over many of the travel and procurement records we had previously requested but had not received.

This was looking way too easy.

Our skepticism was justified when we saw the physical condition of the records. We immediately understood what had happened. The boys had been up all night sanitizing the records.

Some looked like they had been repeatedly sprayed by a shotgun with much of the narrative material cut out. They told us they were ordered to do it by unnamed superiors. They were to only provide us with data on payee, amount, appropriation charged, and certifying officer approval. They were told that we were not authorized to see any of the other data. Of course that is not what our legal authority says—it says we get everything. Unfortunately in those days GAO did not have subpoena power as it does now. We were powerless to do anything unless we wanted to go through the courts, which could take years. But, as often happens during many criminal activities, they were a bit careless.

As I mentioned earlier, it turns out the White House accounting system had been designed some years earlier by several GAO staff. Unchanged, it remained largely a simple manual system. The payroll itself was on another agency's automated system. Payments other than payroll were made by vouchers, the originals of which were sent to the Treasury Department's disbursing center. The center coincidently was located in our headquarters in the GAO office building on G Street. Since payment records were lawfully our "property" we went to the disbursing center and seized the originals of the sanitized records. Of course that action generated another of those calls from Melancamp where I had to hold the phone several inches from my ear.

"You have no damn business taking our records from Treasury and the President wants them returned immediately."

At this point I finally I had had it with his games and I told him if he and the President didn't like it they could sue us. That upset him all the more since White House officials were accustomed to only hearing "yes sir" and "no sir." Melencamp demanded the name of my superior—so I skipped over a few and gave him the Comptroller General's number and suggested he call. He never made the call.

Actually when the smoke cleared, the seized records only filled in some blanks on our audit schedules but did not really provide much useful information. It appeared to us that the weekend sanitizing party was probably a big waste of time but we never passed that on to their staff. Now our problem shifted to another dimension — the Press.

Woodward and Bernstein were beginning to gear up as were some of the TV investigative reporters and several media inquiries were made to the GAO. They were given our normal response that we do not discuss an ongoing investigation, but they kept pushing. At another of those hurried (get your butt over here fast) meetings with the Comptroller General I was told to personally review all GAO work directly or indirectly involving the White House and (lucky me) I was to be the focal point for press contact. Then came a big discovery.

Separately, our Logistics and Communication Division had been reviewing the use of White House aircraft to see if the government was being properly reimbursed for political and personal presidential travel. I began scanning the working papers and there it was. It jumped out and hit me like a brick. Copies of several checks were apparently used to pay for political use of Air Force One. The checks were absolutely plain and bore no imprinted name, organization, or address — just the account number. What hit me was the signature — it was that of Wilbur Jenkins, the White House Administrative officer of 20 plus years — but who held no political position. A quick check with Sam Hughes, the head of the Office of Federal Elections which was then a part of GAO, disclosed that no such account had been reported as required by Federal law.

Naturally this precipitated another fun trip to the White House to see Jenkins. It was a meeting I will never forget. I laid the dozen or so checks down on the table one at a time and asked for a detailed explanation on each. Jenkins was visibly shaken and began to sob. He said he knew he was breaking the law but "they" made him do it if he wanted to keep his job. White House employees, unlike most Government employees, serve at the pleasure of the president. Jenkins then refused to identify who had told him to open the account or provide us with any more information. We turned the information on the account over to the Office of Federal Elections who already had an active investigation going. We went back to trying to complete our work for Sellers.

Unfortunately, the Press did not go away after their initial contacts. After weeks of their continual badgering, I agreed to meet with two reporters from ABC TV. The reporters seemed to be paranoid about meeting in any government facilities, so I met them in a coffee shop on 14th street. From their questions it was clear they were on to what was to become known as the Watergate scandal. But it also was clear that, apparently, they were not willing to invest the time and effort to the same level as Woodward and Bernstein. Too bad. Other than confirming that there was an ongoing investigation, I gave them nothing. I did more listening than talking and they indicated if nothing turned up in a few days they would go on to other assignments.

All of our schedules and document-copying were complete and there would only be one last issue with Sellers. He was now after the "plumbers" and was trying to locate their offices in the Old Executive Office building. Knowing the White House telephone exchange, Sellers began calling every number in sequence trying to obtain the identity and location of the person answering the phone. He spent days and zeroed in on a dozen room numbers. Then came the strangest request from a Congressman's office I had ever heard.

"John, I want you to get some staff over to these rooms at the White House and see who answers the phones."

We were to go to these offices at a specified time and determine who worked there and what they did.

Good grief—what next?

I was sure the Secret Service would not be thrilled with GAO auditors barging into White House offices unannounced. I prepared a polite response for the Comptroller General to explain to Sellers why we did not do that kind of work and set up a meeting. Staats read the incoming letter and as he did I noticed an eyebrow raise. I had learned over the years that was about as severe a reaction as he ever had. He then read my proposed response, told me it was well-written and thanked me for preparing it. He then rolled up both letters into a ball (no shredders in those days) and very quietly said "*that* is our response."

He told me to tell Sellers there would be no GAO response to his request and that we had terminated our work at the White House. I called Sellers and relayed the message with relief and some delight. I honestly was getting a little tired of being harassed and I don't mean just by the press corps. Over the passing weeks Sellers had felt it alright to call me at home at midnight. He usually had questions that could have easily waited to the next day. Lorraine was not pleased.

Sellers' response when I told him we were finished was very brief, he said "don't bet on it" which told me that more trouble was coming. And come it did the next day. An angry Congressmen Burton called Mr. Staats only to find out he was at a meeting of a special procurement commission on which he served. Since the meeting was at the Capitol, the Congressman left his office and headed over to get him out of the meeting. He missed him by ten minutes and went back to his office even angrier. He called Mr. Staats' office and announced he would not get off the phone until he had the Comptroller General on the phone. Aware of what had happened, I was waiting when Staats returned to his office. Congressman Burton had been on hold for about five minutes. Staats listened red-faced to an obvious tirade growing while holding the phone several inches from his ear. Even sitting across the large desk, I could hear the colorful language coming from the receiver.

What happened next showed me what a strong leader Comptroller General Staats was. He could have easily told Burton it was just a misunderstanding—an excuse the White House had proffered—and blame me saying I misquoted him. But to his credit he instead stood firm and acknowledged that that was his personal decision to "pull the plug" since he believed we were going beyond GAO's normal audit function.

He calmed the Congressman down by agreeing to complete the last analysis we had begun preparing. He suggested that future requests come from the House Appropriations Committee as they were the basic oversight committee for White House financing. In fact there wasn't much more we could do on the regular accounts without getting into the secret accounts where it was clear we did not have authority. That situation would change a few years later.

After a few weeks, our work finally was finished but the work of the Congress and many others involved in the Watergate scandal was just beginning. Having described the beginnings of the scandal here, it would serve no useful purpose to rehash the Watergate investigation and hearings as they have been exhaustively covered elsewhere.

It was now December 1972 and thankfully Lorraine and I could focus on Christmas and the new baby. I was pleased and encouraged with the close relationship I had developed with the Comptroller General—a rapport that lasted for years.

2. The Beginning

So how was it that an individual at thirty-eight years of age could take on the President of the United States? I was born in New York City on April 13th, 1934 into a middle-class Irish family. My father had endured a difficult life. He enlisted to serve in World War I at the age of 29 and fought in the major battles. He was severely wounded, and sent home to die—100% disabled. He traveled to Arizona for recovery from his wounds and tuberculosis and somehow managed to beat the odds. He obtained a law degree and returned to New York City. He started a small law practice but lost it in the Depression. He met and married my mother in his mid-40s and of course I came along quickly thereafter.

At about the time I was born, my father began a career with the Veterans Administration. It was not easy starting over at age 45, but he had the courage to persevere despite his poor health. We lived in a two bedroom apartment on the west side of Manhattan. I recall we never went hungry but however we sometimes ate fish more than once a week and not just because we were Catholic. In fact, I grew to hate those nasty little fish called smelts, and I have not had one since I came to Washington sixty years ago.

I went through the parochial school system in New York City

and as the old joke goes, I have the scars to prove it. After graduating from Holy Name Grammar School on West 97th Street in 1947, I attended a Jesuit military high school called St. Francis Xavier. It was a very strict environment and by my junior year, it had become a constant war between Latin and Chemistry and me. I lost the war and transferred to a Christian Brothers School called De La Salle Institute, on West 74th Street. The Jesuits at Xavier were a more conservative, intellectual group and the students worked pretty much independently. The atmosphere at De La Salle was different, and I was able to flourish. The instructors were more encouraging to the point where I made the honor roll, which provided me an easy admission to Manhattan College which was also operated by the Christian Brothers.

As an only child, it was reasonable to describe me as a loner and a little immature. During my last year at De La Salle, I joined the famous Seventh Regiment of the New York National Guard; an action that certainly helped in my maturity and entry into Manhattan College. Manhattan was a college that years earlier had been designed for quality students who could not afford an Ivy League college education. With my background, I certainly fit in that mold very well. Some of my experiences at the Seventh Regiment really opened my eyes and let me see how the other half lived.

Its huge brick building was located right on Park Avenue. We were required to pay dues. We had a company valet to shine our combat boots. It was what one might call a high class military organization and appropriately nicknamed the "silk stocking" regiment. From my military background at Xavier, I was given the opportunity to join the Honor Guard—an elite unit that provided tribute guard and escort services at various high level political and society functions.

These activities gave me a taste of some of the finer things in life that I concluded reasonably that only hard work could provide. I needed to set my goals as high as I could. I had already figured out that New York City was not the best place for me. My father was working hard trying to make ends meet, and now had the added strain of my college costs. I had the routine summer jobs while in high school, but now I figured it was time to support myself as best I could and take some of the financial burden from my father.

As I progressed through Manhattan College, I had several part-time and in some cases full time jobs. I worked as a messenger, dishwasher, lifeguard, swimming instructor, elevator operator and assistant manager of a shoe department. The elevator operator's job was a 66 hours a week job and that took its toll. I had to work from 11:00 at night till 7 a.m., then in the morning I would go off to college. I could sometimes study on the elevator but reversing my days and nights proved too much. Periodically, a professor after class would call me over and slip me some extra reading material to cover the points covered in class since I may have dosed off for a period after running the elevator all night. The faculty at Manhattan College was outstanding at understanding the particular needs of those students who worked.

After four months, I switched into a fairly good job at Brooks Brothers Department Store. I was given the responsibility for maintaining inventory and doing the purchasing and importing for the shoe department. Most importantly, my hours were flexible so I could work around my college schedule.

The job at Brooks Brothers was perhaps the best job of all to prepare me for the early years of my career. Today they call it "dress for success." No, it wasn't the work experience as assistant manager of the shoe department. All I had to do was maintain the inventory and schedule enough lead time so that we could order the imported shoes from England without having an inventory shortage. The best part of the job was the fact that twice a year they would have an employee sale for items taken out of stock. It was called the "TOS" sale. Often, customers with large accounts would return suits and other items of clothing and we accepted them with no questions asked. The suits would be sold to the employees at $10 for suits that were $150 or less and $15 for suits over $150. That was quite a bit of money in those days and very recent college graduates, particularly from the middle class schools, seldom were seen wearing Brooks Brothers suits. I was able to acquire about eight of the suits, along with top coats, hats, and other clothing. This would help me at least look the part despite the lack of resources in the early years of my career.

As spring of 1956 and my graduation approached, it was time to look for a career position. I had majored in accounting. When I had applied for Manhattan College I entered the school of arts and science not knowing which career I wanted to pursue. However, a battery of tests and meetings with counselors, resulted in a suggestion that I study accounting or finance. I enrolled in the school of business and selected accounting as my major. I found that I thoroughly enjoyed the subject and stuck with it for four years — taking every accounting course the college had to offer.

But now, for the difficult problem of finding a job. I still had a number of years to serve in the National Guard or Reserves and worse, was subject to being called to active duty. It quickly became apparent that in the mid-1950s CPA firms were very reluctant to hire any individual with a military obligation. Being a stubborn Irishman, I nevertheless applied to most of the major accounting firms. I decided I wanted to pursue a career in auditing with a possible future move into a corporate accounting position. It was well known that the prestige school at Manhattan was the Engineering School and the engineers were starting out with higher salaries than the accountants. In looking at the long range trends however, it appeared that three to five years out, the accountants had the potential for surpassing the engineers. Although pleased with my selection and my future, I still was not happy with the job prospects.

One of the organizations interviewing the seniors at Manhattan College was something called the General Accounting Office (changed to Government Accountability Office in 2004). They were offering positions based in Washington and at a fairly competitive salary. I signed up for an interview. The two gentlemen that I met described the General Accounting Office as the audit and investigative arm of Congress and offered what appeared to be a very interesting career opportunity. One important thing became clear during the interview. If an individual had a military obligation, that was not a problem. In fact they offered time off for military training. I decided to go for it, with the idea in mind that I would try it for six months to a year in Washington and then try to relocate to another position back in New York. I was pleasantly surprised a few weeks later when I received an appointment letter in the mail appointing me as an accountant/auditor, GS-5, at a salary of $3,670 per year—actually a few dollars less than I was making in the job I had six days a week as an elevator operator. There was however, a promise of a promotion to a GS-7 in six months.

I will always remember the difficulty of telling my mother and father that after so many years I was finally leaving home. I waited till after dinner on the day I had received the job offer and announced that I had found a position and accepted it. My dad asked where I would be working. I told him in an office building on G Street. My father thought for a moment, and looked at me perplexed.

"I don't know of any G Street in New York."

"That's right Dad, this G Street is in Washington!"

I saw a mixture of happiness and possibly a small tear in the corner of his eye. Happiness that I had found a position and would be on my own as an adult and the sadness that comes with the knowledge of generational passage from my leaving home for good. I experienced the same emotion as my oldest son went off to college.

It was August 1957, brutally hot in New York City—probably going to be worse in D.C. My father always put the family car in storage for the winter and only used it for summer trips to nearby beaches and vacations—so I was lucky he let me use it for my trip. I left with good-by waves, tears, and my last one hundred dollars for the five hour drive to Washington.

I decided to locate in less expensive Silver Spring, Maryland, just outside Washington, also so I could also sit for the Certified Public Accountants exam in that State. I arrived early Saturday afternoon, picked up the local paper, and found a furnished room for $35 a month. I knew things would be tight with a take home of about $55 a week. I got settled in and on Monday morning headed for the General Accounting Office. On my arrival, I was sworn in as a federal employee, photographed for credentials, fingerprinted, and provided with an orientation on the General Accounting Office (GAO).

The GAO was then an organization of about 5,000 people, mostly accountants and auditors; about half in Washington and the other half in 15 regional offices around the country. It is headed by the Comptroller General of the United States, who is appointed by the President for a 15 year term and cannot be removed. The purpose of the 15 year term supposedly was to take politics out of the appointment. Thus all Comptroller Generals might serve several administrations. The organization was created in 1921 after several major government scandals such as the Teapot Dome Affair. It provided independent auditing and investigating for the Congress to bolster the system of checks and balances under which our government was formed.

I arrived with a group of about 100. Our training and orientation lasted for three days and took place in a large auditorium in the GAO headquarters building located near the Capitol. The auditorium provided my first culture shock—air conditioning. Having grown up in New York City without any air conditioning except in an occasional movie theater, it was like working in a refrigerator. After about three days I was a basket case. Ears, nose, throat, chest, stopped up to the point where I could hardly breathe. To make matters worse, no doctor and no money to pay for one. Fortunately a federal health unit was kind enough to check me out, give me some basic medication, and send me off to bed for a day or two.

The rest of the entering class had a culture shock a little different than mine. Most of them had come straight from boarding colleges where they also participated in college dorm and fraternity life. I had lived at home—and didn't have the time or money for it anyway. Thus there were many complaints from my associates about adjusting to a 40 hour work week. For me, it was a nice reduction in work hours. Although I didn't immediately realize it, my work habit of staying a little late until I was finished with what I was doing was noticed by my supervisors and started me on a good career path.

So much for my start in the General Accounting Office. In the following chapters I will detail some of the audits and investigations that I was involved in over the succeeding thirty years.

3.My First Audit — A Look At Congressional Perks

Of course, my first assignment looked highly interesting. I was assigned to a group that was responsible for performing financial and other audits of various congressional support activities. I suspected I had been placed on that assignment because the GAO was aware that my grandfather had spent twenty years as a member of Congress. As I soon found out, my grandfather had many friends on Capitol Hill who were still there.

The first audit was of the Sergeant At Arms Congressional Banking Facility. Zeke Johnson, the Sergeant at Arms had been a former Capitol Hill policeman who had become friendly with my grandfather. He had assisted in getting him promoted to his current job, so naturally we started out on very good terms. One early benefit was that even back in the late Fifties, parking in Washington was always difficult. Zeke gave me a special parking permit where I could park right next to the Speaker of the House's parking spot. It was just a few short steps to my office.

Nearby was Zeke's office and the exclusive restaurant reserved for House members. The person in charge of the restaurant was an

elderly woman by the name of Ridgley. She had known my grandfather well. When I introduced myself, she recalled meeting me
when I was a young boy on several of the trips I took to Washington with my grandfather. She was a very gracious lady and also offered me a very special perk; the use of the members dining room.

Perks are for everyone!

Starting a financial audit can be pretty routine. The auditor
generally compares prior reports, information on the operation
being audited, and the prior audit workpapers. The big difference
between an average auditor and a good auditor is inquisitiveness.
An average auditor will go through the records with the objective of showing that everything is right. A good auditor (even a
good government auditor) has a certain curiosity. The good auditor
should constantly probe to see what, if anything, may be wrong. It
didn't take long for a problem to surface.

The Sergeant at Arms operates a banking facility in a fashion
very similar to a commercial bank except that the only customers
are members of Congress. In those days in the commercial sector, most people had checking accounts where they paid a small
monthly fee of 50 cents and paid a charge for each check—usually about 10 cents. Not so for the members of Congress, their
checking was free and unlimited. But I noticed something that
looked rather peculiar in the records and prior statements. There
was a classification similar to an account receivable called "Hold
Checks." As I started reviewing the details of the accounts, it became obvious what these checks were. They were checks written in
excess of the Congressman's available funds in his account. They
were basically "bounced" checks, but the checks were not bounced.
They were just paid and covered over by the balances in the other
Congressional checking accounts. This way the Bank itself was always balanced even if the individual accounts were not.

Apparently members were routinely allowed to bounce checks for up to one month's salary. If the amount of the insufficient funds exceeded the salary amount due the following month something amazing happened. That something turned out to be a free subsidized loan from the National Bank of Washington. Conveniently, the head teller at the Congressional Banking Facility was also an appointed loan officer of the National Bank of Washington. He would automatically process a loan document advancing the member one month's salary. There would be no interest on the loan.

Pretty smooth operation.

The records showed a number of the members were behind thousands and thousands of dollars. I asked for access to the loan portfolios, but the Chief Teller and the Sergeant at Arms denied the request saying that was not a function of the audit. They took the position I was to limit myself to the books and records of the Congressional Bank, *not* including the loan records of the local bank providing the loans.

Naturally that merely created an additional step and only made me work harder. It was relatively easy to go through the accounts and reconstruct where the loans were deposited into the members account. There would usually be an entry amount about equal to the members' monthly salary followed by a record of bounced checks that had been paid. Except for this issue, the rest of the audit was pretty straightforward.

Now the important question became how to present my findings to my superiors in the General Accounting Office. Obviously, these issues were examined before. They were disclosed in prior reports—but not as bounced checks, merely as an account receivable. And there were never any references to the interest free loans. Thus, even on my first audit I began my career as troublemaker.

Low man on the totem pole, I was reporting to an Audit

Supervisor who was reporting to a Senior Audit Manager. The manager decided to visit the audit site one day which gave me my opportunity. The Audit Manager, Charles Iovino, was the first CPA hired by GAO. After World War II, the GAO had reorganized itself. Prior to that time, it was a very large organization in excess of 16,000 employees. After World War II many of its basic auditing functions were transferred back into the executive agencies. The GAO had the biggest reduction in force in its history. They went from 16,000 down to its present size of about 5,000. More importantly, it began to bring in CPAs and upgrade itself into the current auditing and investigative organization it is known as today.

Iovino visited the audit site with me to review my work. He was a famous CPA. He was the only congressional accountant that knew about the Manhattan project in World War II that developed the atomic bomb. He knew more details than Vice President Truman and did an outstanding job of reviewing contracts and security measures. Further, he had no idea of my grandfather's history and my relationships on the Hill.

When he arrived at the Congressional Bank in the early afternoon, I was having a late lunch, having had some lengthy staff discussions about the bounced checks. He was directed to the members' dining room where I was just finishing up. With my back to the entrance, I did not see him. Fortunately, my friend and protector, Mrs. Ridgley did. She rushed over, grabbed him by the arm and proceeded to escort him out of the dining room.

Somewhat upset, he explained to her he was looking for me and that he was my boss. Mrs. Ridgley, unimpressed as usual, made him wait in the hall while she came over and told me about the gentleman that was trying to see me. I finally turned around, took one look at my boss's face and knew then and there I was in trouble. Again, Mrs. Ridgley the true politician came to my rescue. She sensed the problem and immediately bought Iovino into the dining room, got him a cup of coffee, and profusely apologized for escorting him out.

I sat down and while Iovino was still in a state of shock, I decided to drop the bomb about the bounced checks. He said he was aware of the problem. I told him that I thought the report should be changed from the easy pass given in prior years. Also, that the problem should be disclosed with a recommendation that the custom be discontinued because they were not accepted or proper banking practices. Congressmen should be held to the same basic standards as the rest of the public. Iovino clearly became a little uptight and immediately suggested we withdraw to the GAO.

We first returned to the Bank where I packed up my papers and then left the facility. I suggested we drive. We walked out the front door of the Capitol and down the steps. An awaiting police officer gave me a friendly good afternoon as I entered my car parked next to the Speakers car. Well, I guess that was too much for Iovino. He just looked at me and said, "Cronin, what the hell is going on here?" I stumbled through the explanation about my grandfather and his relationship with Mrs. Ridgley and Sergeant at Arms. I guess it settled Iovino down, but not much was said on the trip back to the GAO.

We went to his office where a heated discussion immediately started on the matter of how the checks would be reported. He took the position of defending the prior reports and stated forcefully that we would not be making a recommendation to discontinue the practice. After further discussions, he relented and agreed that we could make a somewhat more accurate disclosure of the exact status of the checks and what they represented.

Since I had a career in front of me and didn't want to "rock the boat" this seemed to be a victory of sort. It also became very clear that I needed to be very careful with our relations with Congress. The GAO's independence was established distinctly with regard to the Executive Branch. But care had to be exercised not to upset members of Congress who had the direct power to make life difficult for the GAO.

Once the audit was complete, I drafted the report language disclosing the practice of the bad checks. I prepared it using some fairly strong language. I did not use the word "bad" or "bounced" checks but merely called them insufficient funds checks. Even that term did not last very long, but a compromise was reached to disclose only the overdraft practice itself. No mention was made however, of the loans from the banking institution. The report simply stated that covering deposits were usually made by the first of the following month.

Consider me schooled…

I suppose this was a small victory, but over the years I would watch my agency grow in stature and in its ability to take on difficult and substantial political issues both with Congress and with the Executive Branch. Basically, just more ways for me to get into trouble.

4. The Federal Meat Inspection Scandal

How do you like your steak? Medium rare, with a little béarnaise sauce on the side, or filthy with a little tuberculosis? Chances are you may be getting both.

In 1958 my tour of the Capitol Hill audits completed, the GAO reassigned me to a two-year assignment at the Department of Agriculture. Specifically, I reported to the audit staff at the Agriculture Research Service. The Audit Manager in charge was Bill Henry, while Don Joseph was my immediate supervisor. My first job was to help in the preparation of a report on the Agricultural Research Service—Meat Inspection Division. That organization was responsible for carrying out sanitary inspections at over 1300 slaughtering, meat canning, packing, and rendering plants nation-wide.

At this point, the GAO was still in the process of converting from purely financial auditing to what was called comprehensive auditing. That meant reviewing the complete operations of various programs and activities of the federal agencies. We were to see not only that they were spending the money correctly but also that they were performing their duties in accordance with the basic responsibilities as laid out by the enabling laws passed by Congress. In those early days, GAO's ability to evaluate federal programs would be frequently (and jealously) challenged. The basis of the challenge typically would be "how can you accountants evaluate the activities of our technical experts?" In the case of the veterinarians who were meat inspectors, it was easy. We found that supervisors were the ones actually preparing the final reports, based on the vets' personal visits to meat inspection plants. Unfortunately, we found also that nothing was ever happening with the on-site recommendations contained in those reports.

Our field office audit team obtained about seventy comprehensive veterinarians' supervisory investigation reports covering over two hundred fifty meat packing establishments. The practices and conditions detailed in the site reports were horrible. Although initially we could not develop any direct evidence on the causes, we were informed that one of the reasons the final reports were whitewashed was pressure from the meat industry. In order to save money, corners were cut. Often large meat packers working through their Congressmen would bring pressure to bear on the Agriculture Research Service to ease up on enforcement. This made it particularly difficult for any low-paid meat inspectors desiring to hold on to their jobs.

Many of the inspector reports we reviewed covered the training of veterinarians and inspectors. In some cases, it had been reported that inspectors assigned to sausage departments were not fully informed of the proper procedure to be followed in the processing of sausage. Additional comments to the effect that the inspector was not sufficiently aware of such things as the ingredients of the product, nor was the labeling of the sausage properly controlled. Many product inspectors obviously were in need of additional training.

The GAO being a very conservative organization, had a Policy, Report, and Review Department that carefully scrutinized all reports. Its main purpose was to make certain all reports were accurate, fair, and objective. A hard-hitting report that might appear to have a degree of sensationalism would always be trouble. Naturally, our report was trouble and was flagged.

I like trouble…

We felt it necessary to include in our report fairly vivid descriptions of the unsanitary conditions found at many of the plants. Diseased meat and meat products were found everywhere. Meat products were prepared and packed in extremely unsanitary conditions. The most common practice was to process an animal that had tuberculosis and send the diseased meat on to final processing rather than totally destroying the animal as required by law.

As a consequence of the revelations, almost immediately our team was called to the office of Policy, Report, and Review for an urgent meeting. Talking to my supervisor, I suggested that it might be good to schedule the meeting right after lunch and take a number of inspection reports with us—along with a selection of damning photographs. I had one particular report in mind. It described leaky pipes directly over a meat processing area. The pipes happened to be the sewage pipes coming from a toilet on the second floor. We let the reviewer read the report. He had finished lunch about 20 minutes earlier. After reading the report, he did not look well. I told him we had several more reports we would like him to read. He read them over very quickly, and we reached a swift compromise. The language we agreed upon in our report to the Congress was as follows:

"At two establishments we noted poor housekeeping, lack of cleanliness, and conditions that were considered unsanitary. These conditions consisted of rusty pipes and condensation on overhead structures where prepared food was stored in open containers; traces of food particles on low ceilings; cartons, containers, casings, and labels stacked in various locations throughout the plant. Accumulations of trash in corners and out-of-the-way places; scraps of meat, paper, and wood in a cage used to retain meat pressed for cooking or refrigeration; cutting boards which were worn and contained holes and splits; and a dirty and oily overhead mechanism on an elevator used to haul meat carcasses."

In summary, the reports disclosed that terribly unsanitary conditions were found in 120 of the 255 establishments covered.

Our Final Report was issued in June of 1959. It created quite a stir. People commented both positively and negatively, both inside and outside of GAO. I was reasonably pleased with how our findings in the report were received. Unfortunately, at this point in history the GAO was not very adept at dealing with the press — meaning how to use them to our advantage. That would change in years to come. This particular report only got a bit of press coverage but the meat packing industry went on the attack. We had dozens of calls from members of Congress for meetings and briefings which we held, armed with our inspection reports. Many of the Members promised to create Congressional oversight of the meat packing industry to assure that conditions were improved. Even the officials of the Agriculture Research Service promised to do a better job and that conditions would improve. We also met directly with executives of the meat packing and meat processing industries. They all were appalled and promised to take steps to see that conditions would improve.

Yeah, right...

They were all empty promises. Conditions did not improve, and as subsequent investigations would show, conditions in fact got worse. About 10 years had passed and I was on a different assignment, but new GAO audit concepts and procedures now were in place at the Department of Agriculture. It was called a Troika. Previously, audit staffs were assigned to each major segment of a department and would be responsible for all phases of an audit. In the new Troika system, three senior people were assigned to the department. One would handle audit planning, a second would handle the management of the field audit, and a third would handle reporting. A good friend of mine, Bill Martin, was now in charge of planning. He knew that I had worked on the Agriculture audit years earlier and I had told him about the meat inspection problem. He asked me to join his team. Prior to beginning his new audit, Bill also talked to many others, then began his research. One of the elements that kept coming up was that the meat inspection problem had probably gotten worse.

Bill's audit was done a little differently than our earlier audits. Key to this was that we were learning to develop our own internal expertise. We devised scientific data collection instruments and our auditors received instructions on investigative procedures to identify meat contamination. In this project, GAO auditors visited forty plants around the country. To no one's surprise, we found unsanitary conditions that would easily result in product contamination at thirty-six of the plants. At thirty of the plants there was definite evidence of long-standing, prior contamination.

What made the situation even more aggravating was that not only did our 1959 report identify all these problems, but other audits did as well. Over the years in the Executive Branch, the Inspector General concept had grown up and was now widely accepted. Most agencies now had an internal audit function, and in many cases the function was decentralized. Since 1978, this has been controlled by statute.

Our new report began by commenting on the Inspector General's activities, and in fact referenced a 1965 report where the IG detailed the existence of contaminated conditions in a number of meat plants. The report identified many types of unsanitary conditions such as inadequate vermin control, unclean saws and meat carts, flaking paint directly over exposed meat, and dropping meat products on the floor. The reports concluded that a passive attitude on the part of meat inspectors, a general reluctance to incur the displeasure of plant management, and a lack of uniformity in the enforcement of sanitary requirements contributed to the deplorable conditions. Four years later, in 1969, the office of Inspector General had issued another report citing the continued existence of the same problems.

Our report came out in June 1970, and history repeats itself. In the thirty plants where unsanitary conditions and product contamination were directly observed, things were just as bad as they were in 1958. The change was however, that GAO had become less conservative. The identical conditions now were described more vividly. We reported the following:

"Contaminants observed in the plants included fecal material, stomach contents, hair, rust, and condensation everywhere. Potential contamination was evidence by desecrated floors, walls, and overhead structures; rusty equipment; generally unapproved sanitation, and inadequately cleaned equipment. Obvious evidence of inadequate pest control was observed in 27 of the plants. Inside two of the plants, GAO investigators observed live rodents. At one of these plants, observations were made that rodents had contaminated unwrapped cheese stored for use in meat/cheese products. Other observations showed evidence of rodents, primarily rodent feces, inside five additional plants. At seven other plants, live rodents were observed on the outside premises or areas of where inedible products were processed."

Not very appetizing…

In reporting these conditions, it was clear they were the same or worse than we reported in 1958. However, notice the language used in the reports. No longer did we use soft general terms as "leaky or rusty pipes." We now were identifying what was leaking out of the pipes and directly into the food products.

Where do we stand today? I believe things are getting worse or at least no better—but for another reason. Modern technology provides ranchers raising cattle and other animals for slaughter opportunities to avoid disease and fatten cattle up by the use of drugs and chemicals. Today, steroids and antibiotics are in wide use in animals. Take, for example, penicillin. Penicillin, like steroids and other medications, is impossible to detect the way our current meat inspection system operates. Many people are extremely allergic to penicillin. Many animals receive penicillin in large doses to clear up infection or avoid a particular illness. The penicillin is carried over into the meat that we eat. A steak heavily laden with penicillin can easily cause difficulty to an individual extremely allergic to that drug.

Forty years later, what have we learned from all of this? Over and over—decade after decade—a federal agency charged with protecting the public is unwilling to do its job. Often, they are hampered by pressures from major industries such as the meat packing industry. Unfortunately, there is also a lack of strong, consistent leadership from the top at the Department of Agriculture, Congress, or even the White House. Often top executives are appointed directly from the industries that they are supposed to regulate. This, coupled with the fact that the average top political appointee only spends less than 18 months in office, it is difficult to provide consistent enforcement. So, when you eat your next steak, you might ask yourself the question, "Was this processed in a good plant or in one of the more than half of the unsanitary plants in the nation?"

5. The Banking Industry's Great Treasury Raid Of The 60'S

It was now January 1962 and my Agriculture Department work was over. There were fifteen regular operating grades in government, and I had been promoted to GS-11, not bad in five years. I was tracking quite well compared to my classmates and was anxiously awaiting my new assignment that would possibly give me the opportunity to demonstrate my skills and move into the supervisory level of GS-12.

As was customary, I reported to the Office of the Director first thing on a Monday morning to find out where I would be assigned. The Director told me I was going to do the Treasury Department audits. He said I would work in the financial area; an area in which they recently had given a high priority, and that I would be given the opportunity for supervision. What I did not know was that I was in for a lucky break.

I hopped in a cab and endured the D.C traffic for forty-five minutes in a trip that should take ten. I went cross town to the Treasury Department which was located across the street from the White House. There I met with the Assistant Director, Otis

McDowell. He told me I was going to the financial side of the treasury audits, overseeing the Office of the Treasurer of the United States, AND that the GS-12 supervisor for whom I was to work had suddenly resigned a week earlier. Given that they would not be able to fill that position right away and that I was to be the number two person on the job, I should take over in charge of the audit site. Not only had I just moved to a supervisory level, I was now on the list of the 40 plus audit site supervisors in the much sought after Washington area. I was the first of my class to be listed as a site supervisor.

That was the good news. The bad news was that there were six of us crammed into audit site offices in a horrible location and covered with filth. Understand that frequently GAO auditors are not treated very well by departments and agencies. They felt we were only there to make trouble for them. They generally provided us with audit space, but quite often it was the worst available. I guess this was understandable because they didn't want us snooping around in the first place — so why make us comfortable. In this instance, the Treasury Department outdid themselves.

Our "workspace" was a section of a dirty old file room from which several rows of file cabinets had been removed. A bunch of desks had been shoved into the area. There were no windows, air circulation was non-existent, and old fashioned light bulbs with metal shades dangled from the high ceiling. In fact, this converted storage area was located right *under* the marble steps that led from Pennsylvania Avenue to the main Treasury Department entrance.

Since this was my first leadership assignment, I decided not to make waves and make the best of it. I would concentrate on convincing the Assistant Director that I was capable of running the best damn audit he had ever seen.

I understood that the recurring financial audit of the Office of the Treasurer was always a challenging audit. Required by statue, in its largest sense it comprised of a review of the balance sheet and income statement of the entire federal government. Our job was to do a CPA type audit and render an opinion to the Congress on the accuracy of the financial statements. We listed all the assets—gold, silver, cash, as well as liabilities in the form of the public debt. Then, similarly to your personal checking account, we reconciled the income and the expenditures of the entire federal government. One benefit of the sheer magnitude of the project was that the audit could be easily separated into a number of segments.

The various bond accounts, receivables, gold accounts, and others were easily isolated for training purposes so that some of my new GAO auditors could be assigned on a piece-work basis. The concept was that every new GAO auditor in his or her first year would be assigned to this part of the audit for two months. That gave me the perfect opportunity to provide the Director's Office with immediate feedback on my supervisory skills. It also helped to increase my confidence level in managing and supervising. This experience would really pay off in years to come.

In our pre-audit strategy sessions, I discussed the issues with the staff. In carefully reviewing the accounts, a number of practices I observed just didn't seem right. In fact, disagreements over these issues between the GAO and the Treasury Department would continue for years.

I had three basic areas of concern, (1) the existence of confederate war bonds on the books of the United States of America, (2) the presence of tens of millions of dollars of savings bonds belonging to World War II veterans, and (3) the nation's income tax collections being held in banks without interest. Although the third point is by far the larger one by dollar amount, let me address the first two initially.

Amongst its many responsibilities, the Treasurer of the United States held in safe keeping various securities including the capital stock of government corporations, the Federal Deposit Insurance Corporation, and other federal organizations. I noted there was one category of the securities in safe keeping called "Other." It was an entry for sixty-four million dollars of face value of securities. The account at least was footnoted to show the securities were stated at face value and did not represent or bear any relationship to the current value of the securities. But it did not state that any of them were worthless or for that matter, priceless.

In reviewing the details of the "Other" account, we noted about 10 million dollars of the securities were called "State of Louisiana Security Bonds. They were dated in the year of 1862. With some quick research it didn't take me long to realize that these were probably Confederate War Bonds. I decided to visit the safe keeping department and asked to look at the securities. The people responsible for the vault got a strange look on their face and initially were reluctant to provide me the information. I pointed out to them something they knew—I had a legal right of access. I went into the vault and looked at the records and that's exactly what they were, Confederate War Bonds. In fact they had been captured in General Sherman's march to the sea in late December, 1864. They were turned over to the U.S. War Department, who turned them over to the Treasurer of the United States.

For the last 100 years, the Treasury Department could not figure out what to do with them except to put them on their financial statements—God only knows why. It made me think of the interesting disclosure we could make and even use a popular phrase in our report, "Save your confederate money, boys, the South will rise again." My humor did not go over too well with my supervisors. Nevertheless, I thought that given the erroneous balance sheet entry, we should make a disclosure about the worthless bonds in our report. I got nowhere and was told there would be no changes from the previous report. I was a little frustrated, but at this point I was not going to make waves that could affect my career over such an unimportant item.

A similar valuation situation happened regarding the Veterans' Savings Bonds. The Office of the Treasurer held about $50 million dollars of savings bonds that had belonged to World War II veterans. In looking at those records it was clear that there had been no activity in these accounts since the end of the war. In some cases, the Treasury Department had been notified that the service man was killed in action. Treasury believed they were bankers with a fiduciary relationship only, merely custodians and nothing more. They said they had no responsibility to initiate any action to return the money. I felt otherwise.

The bonds were issued by the government but did not belong to the government. They should not have been carried on their balance sheet as an asset. In fact, they were liabilities, debts of the government, owed to their citizen-owners who had lent them the money by purchasing the bonds in the first place.

The audit team debated the concerns and decided that Treasury should take some action to get the bonds back to their rightful owners or heirs—and with any luck, with interest! I took the problem up with the Assistant Director as well as at some higher levels of GAO.

We were stonewalled. In those days, the basic protocol was that if we found an error where the government *lost* money, we were to pursue it, but as in this case, if we found an error in the government's favor, we were to keep our mouths shut. There was actually a statute on the books that forbade inviting a claim against the government. The view in those days was that such action would invite a claim regardless of whether the service man was entitled to the proceeds or not. Actually, as described later on in this book, ten years later in fact, the issue would surface again, and the veterans finally would receive their just due.

Anyway, I had just lost round two.

The third and substantially larger issue that we next concentrated on pertained to nothing less than the nations' tax collection system. Billions of dollars of annual tax collections from both corporations and individuals were collected through the U.S. banking system. The monies included individual payroll taxes as well as corporation and business taxes. An employer after taking the tax withholding of its workers or filing other tax returns, would regularly deposit these amounts in their local bank into a special treasury account. In 1962, about 11,000 of the 16,000 banks in the nation maintained such accounts. The cash would sit on deposit in these accounts until called upon by the Treasury Department to cover its expenditures. Treasury anticipated the need for cash and transferred these tax receipts into its various operating accounts at the Federal Reserve Banks. Depending upon the time of the year, the balance in these accounts ranged between three and six billion dollars—a LOT of money over fifty years ago. Over half of the funds were on deposit in the top sixty of the national banks.

And why should this be a concern? Because the banks paid no interest to the government on these funds. They had in a sense the free use of the money for whatever purposes they desired until they were called by the Treasury Department. Naturally however, there would be ample notice, so the banks could liquidate whatever they needed to produce the funds. Also, there was a law saying that individual checking accounts could not pay interest. That never made any sense to me either—but of course I was not part of the powerful banking lobby.

My audit team became convinced that the law should be changed. I believed the Treasury should at least earn some interest on these funds. After all, the banks were earning large profits investing and loaning these funds. We put in our audit report a recommendation of remedy that would be repeated in the GAO Annual Report on the Treasury for many years. I guess the battle lasted for well over ten years—with no action.

We also did a special study, an analysis of this income as derived by banks. Treasury responded with a study and report of their own. Treasury's rather weak argument was that the banks performed services for them, and these deposits acted as "compensating balances" for those services. Actually, there were other deposits in the banks called time deposits to reimburse the banks. Their other argument was that banks sold and redeemed savings bonds for the government and the banks ought to have those funds available to compensate them for that. GAO, however, took the position that selling savings bonds, while providing some benefit to the federal government, provided a huge benefit to the banks in terms of a service for depositors. Redeeming savings bonds was a somewhat ridiculous argument since when a bank received a bond, it was paid a service fee on top for each bond redeemed.

Initially it was difficult to understand the rationale behind Treasury's position. That was until one examined the top Treasury personnel. One of the key positions in Treasury has always been the Fiscal Assistant Secretary.

During a large portion of this time frame, this position was held by William Hefflefinger. When Mr. Hefflefinger retired from the Treasury Department, he accepted a lucrative position with the American Bankers Association. There appeared to be a case of the preverbal "revolving door" between banking industry executives and the Treasury Department. Our research showed that there were not many arms-length dealings between them. I also noted that despite numerous GAO alerts over the years, Congress remained reluctant to step into this battle. They did not wish to jump into what they felt was a technical issue between the accountants of GAO, the bankers, and the Treasury Department.

Well, it did take about 10 years, and while I was no longer on the Treasury assignment, GAO finally persevered. It took the enormously rising interest rates of the '70s and a crashing economy for the Treasury Department to back down on its position. The political pressure was so great that they finally agreed and worked things out. Now, the banks were paying interest on the tax and loan account balances—which of course had also grown exponentially. Treasury still took a final shot at GAO. They said they only were doing this because of changing economic conditions and in no way it was related to the position taken in the years of GAO criticism.

If anybody believes that, I would be happy to sell them some stock in the Brooklyn Bridge.

Despite some personal disappointment that I had not been able to change the world, at least my career was moving along nicely. The issues I had raised at Treasury, together with my successful completion of another career goal, passing the Certified Public Accountants examination in Maryland, had been brought to the attention of my supervisors. I was suddenly promoted to a GS-12 supervisor and starting to move well ahead of my classmates. Often within an assignment area as large and complex as the Treasury Department, supervisors would move as well. So with my new GS-12 paperwork in hand I was asked to take over the audits of the Bureau of Engraving and Printing, the organization that manufactures the nation's currency and postage stamps. That too was a challenge and a very interesting assignment.

In a sense, I was again totally on my own. Interestingly enough, my boss was the Harold I mentioned earlier in this book who had a serious drinking problem. At Treasury, few senior supervisory visits were paid due to the high security. Because of this, Harold and *his* supervisor were required to make an appointment to visit the audit—so I didn't see much of them. Within the facility I had a special badge that enabled free access throughout the complex, but staffers were required to remain in their particular work area.

During this period there were several interesting government accounting issues that I had to deal with but will not bore the reader with their intricacies here. But one problem scenario, however, will show how things sometimes work in a bureaucracy.

Periodically I was asked to lecture to our incoming trainee auditors. I would give them a rather technical lecture and overview on how the government's accounting and financial management systems worked. That by itself could be a very boring subject—particularly for the know-it-all newbies. As I had done some teaching before, I always liked to liven up my classes with interesting stories or exhibits. One of the popular financial frauds of the day was for individuals with access to corporate bond records to remove bearer bond coupons due in future periods and substitute bogus counterfeit securities. The bearer bonds would then be sold, and the bogus securities would not be discovered until the redemption time—sometimes years later.

For my class I thought it would be interesting to obtain some seized counterfeit money from the Treasury Department. I would just pass it around and let the students see what counterfeit bills looked like. Since I had a number of dealings with the Secret Service while I did the accounts of the Treasury Office, I borrowed some counterfeit money for my lecture. Of course, officially they steadfastly maintained that would be unlawful for me to do. But they did want to help so they provided me with some props and some nice exhibits. They gave me some overhead enlargements that showed the difference between the legitimate Treasury seal on our currency and a bogus seal, as well as the difference between legitimate and bogus currency portraits. Then I stopped over at the research and development section of the Bureau of Engraving and Printing and made the same inquiry. They too agreed to help. They had a supply of various counterfeit bills on hand. I merely had to sign a receipt stating what the bills would be used for and promise to return them after the lecture. They did have some concerns about my use of portraits and seals because they could be used by potential counterfeiters, but I promised to be a good boy and take care of them.

So for several years on the day prior to my lecture, I would visit the Secret Service and obtain their portraits and seals and then go down the street to the Bureau of Engraving and Printing and obtain the counterfeit bills. I suspect that when my old friends at the Treasury Department finish reading this passage, someone will say, "That son of a bitch pulled another fast one."

6. The National Park System—The Taxpayer Loses Again

For those that have visited some of our nation's largest national parks you probably had a very enjoyable time. Yosemite, Grand Canyon, Yellowstone, and other magnificent national treasures and are certainly beautiful locations to visit. If there was one negative aspect many of you would share, it might be the large hole in your wallet after spending some time in one of the parks.

The weightlessness of your wallet might be attributed to the outrageous charges and resultant profits made by concessionaires in the National Park system. Unfortunately, the National Park Service (NPS) has a history of turning its back on financial abuses. One would ask why? The answer is simple. A powerful political organization of concessionaires in the 1960's engaged in a program of heavy lobbying among sympathetic Congressmen on the Interior and Insular Affairs Committee.

This is how the scam worked that allowed the NPS and you, the public, to get hoodwinked. The Service makes an announcement that a contract is available for the operation of a particular park concession facility. It could be a hotel, restaurant, store, gas station, etc. If it is a brand-new application, the concessioner is required to construct the facility. Once granted, the concessioner obviously has a titular interest in the facility they construct, and he usually retains that contract "forever" with periodic renegotiations. If a concessionaire is to change, there is a negotiated settlement agreed to between the private parties—old concessionaire and new concessionaire. The NPS is pretty much on the sideline but retains the option of approving the amounts to be charged. One could liken the approval of the rates to a gigantic tug of war with the NPS always losing.

It was now 1963, and having finished my tour at Treasury, I was transferred to our GAO audit site at the Department of the Interior. I was given responsibility for two agencies, the National Park Service and Bureau of Outdoor Recreation. This was another move upward. I was pleased because I was replacing a GS-13 who was transferring. Again, that gave me more opportunity to demonstrate broader management skills, since much of the work now involved managing teams out of our regional offices around the country. My predecessor had started a review of the NPS concession policies in the parks and it was my job to finish the review and issue the final report to Congress. Now, I was in a position where I was reporting directly to an Assistant Director, Bill Parker. After I had a detailed briefing on the job, he gave it to me pretty straight.

"John, we may be in a hell of a lot of trouble on this one."

He told me that the Interior and Insular Affairs Committee of the House of Representatives was a little too supportive of one of the most powerful concessionaires in the park system, the Yosemite Park and Curry Company. He indicated that one particular Committee member from Pennsylvania, John Saylor, was a strong supporter of the concessionaire, even though he had no national parks in his district.

From the name of the company, it was obvious they had started their concession activities at Yosemite—one of the largest and most visited parks in the system. Over the years the Company had branched out into a number of the other large national parks around the country. We began our research and quickly realized that the Yosemite Park and Curry Company was almost the only concessionaire in the Park.

They had a contract for operation of the main lodge, the restaurants, the service stations, and other facilities. They had negotiated a very favorable concession fee with NPS. The fee was an outrageous rip off of the government and the taxpayer. Ostensively the fee was to cover the privilege of being in the park, and to cover services provided to them by the NPS. Not only was the facility inside a National Park but the NPS also provided police and fire protection, water and sewage, not to mention the extensive national advertising the government provides to support the park system.

The most outrageous abuse we found at Yosemite pertained to the company's subcontracting procedures. After negotiating the base fee, they paid the Park Service for the umbrella concession, they then turned around and negotiated a subcontract with the Exxon Oil Company to operate the gasoline stations inside the park. The concession fee they were paid by Exxon actually was higher than the total fee they paid to the government for the base concession facilities umbrella. They even negotiated a cut for themselves on the gasoline sales.

The primary person responsible for evaluating the prices charged by the concessionaire was the individual park superintendent. Being a park superintendent was not an easy job. The pay was not outstanding, and the responsibilities were awesome. He was like the mayor of a large city—responsible for police, fire, safety, all administrative staff, construction, facility maintenance, collection of fees, and so on. All this AND overseeing the concession facilities at the park. None of the park superintendents were accountants, had financial backgrounds, or were even experienced contract negotiators. Washington did have a concession policy office that was available to provide some assistance to park superintendents. But for most major contracts, the superintendents were on their own.

When my auditors began to question a number of the rates charged and the profits being made by the concessionaires, we had a strangely difficult time gaining access to the actual records. We were told by the concessionaires that their rates were higher because of the isolated location of the parks. They frequently cited the difficulty of getting food and supplies as well as the seasonal nature of their activities.

Well, we asked ourselves a simple question. How then do the businesses just outside the park operate given they are basically in the same location? We started making some comparisons of meal prices, hotel rates, gasoline prices, grocery prices, etc. We found that the prices outside the park were thirty to forty percent lower. In theory, if the facilities were equal, the prices outside the park should have been higher. The businessmen outside the park have to pay the wide range of taxes to the local community and state, from which most concessionaires are exempt. The businesses outside the park faced the same problems with logistics and the seasonal nature of the activity since they were at the same location usually just outside or not far from the park entrance. They would often handle the overflow crowd or served those citizens who simply could not afford to stay inside the park.

The fee-setting process was bad enough. We then uncovered another opportunity for the concessionaires to scam another big victory at the expense of the taxpayer. At contract renewal time for a concession, other would-be concessionaires could offer a bid to the Park Service on the basis of the prices they would charge and the concession fees that they would pay. If the Park Service decided to select a new concessionaire, there would have to be a negotiation with the existing concessionaire. An agreement had to be reached on the price to be paid for the assets that had been developed in the park. This would usually result in a big battle.

To help protect their interests, the Yosemite Park and Curry Company led the charge to pass a piece of legislation called the Concession Policy Bill. First it labeled the original concessionaire's investment as a "possessory interest." The bill said that an incoming concessionaire would have to buy out the possessory interest of the existing concessionaire. The catch of course was, it allowed the departing concessionaire to set its own value on the possessory interest, and thus could then take into consideration such vague accounting items as the increase in goodwill established over the years. Pretty good deal for the concessionaire, but a bad deal for the government and the taxpayer.

My staff and I eagerly took on this blatant taxpayer rip-off. Unfortunately in the process, the GAO took about the worst beating from the Congress that I had ever seen. It was also the first time I saw two major committees on the Hill "fight it out."

The Appropriations Committee loved our report and the issues we had raised regarding the park concessionaires. The Interior and Insular Affairs Committee, however, took a position supporting the status quo. Appropriations even prepared ten recommendations which they sent directly to the Park Service and to the Interior and Insular Affairs Committee. The Appropriations Committee was concerned about the extent of the various "subsidies" granted, while so little was being recovered due to the concession fees being so badly negotiated. The Interior Committee cleverly managed to put us square in the middle.

Most Congressional committees are very supportive of the work of the GAO and our ability to ferret out fraud, waste, and abuse. Our prominence at Congressional hearings at which federal agencies and government contractors are asked to testify played well politically for the folks at home. Interior sent us the ten recommendations of the Appropriations Committee and asked us for our opinion on each recommendation. GAO reports and testimonies are used to institute legislative or other corrective actions.

We sent out another report strongly agreeing with nine of the recommendations and taking no position on the last. This infuriated the Interior and Insular Affairs Committee in general, and in particular, Congressman John Saylor.

We found ourselves being called on the carpet by the Interior and Insular Affairs Committee to be chastised for somehow "interfering" with the operations of the National Park System. At the ensuing congressional hearing, GAO's witness in this case was Bill Parker, our Assistant Director. Witnesses first read an opening statement which is placed into the record. The Committee was not even happy with our opening statement and did not let Parker get through his opening remarks before they started rebuking us for our report and the issues we had raised. They classified our report in terms such as "irresponsible" and yet said many glowing things about how the concessionaires were helping the American people enjoy the national parks.

We wanted to throw up.

The ensuing "dialogue" got us absolutely nowhere. When we would answer the disparaging questions posed by Congressman Saylor, we often referred to how differently concession policies are granted in his home state of Pennsylvania such as for the facilities on the Pennsylvania Turnpike. We had some good ammunition. The turnpike concessions were heavily scrutinized and were at arm's length — thanks to the efforts at the State level. Our ammunition was so good, in fact, that when the hearings were printed, some of our answers had been completely removed from the record. No action was taken by any of the Committee members for changes or even a reprimand.

The hearing over, and as the old expression goes, we washed off the blood, changed our clothes, and went back to our offices at GAO to continue our efforts as best as we could. The lobbyists were just too powerful.

Fortunately, such activities would probably not happen as easily in the current Congressional environment. Today, individual Congressional financing and reelection campaign financing ties are closely watched. The press and the public are on alert for conflicts of interest between members of Congress and groups they regulate. The damage to the National Park system, however, was done and remains somewhat even today. The park superintendents are still overwhelmed with all their responsibilities and their low salaries.

My recommendation for the best way for the taxpayer to avoid the hole in their wallet at the parks is by all means visit them; but patronize the businesses outside the parks. Our National Parks are very beautiful, but if you stay outside the parks and spend as little cash as possible inside the parks, it might discourage the concessioners from further abuses.

7. Feeding At The Federal Grant Trough
—Or—
How Not To Play Politics

After the frustration of taking on the concessionaires inside the National Parks, things had settled down and were running nicely with my responsibilities for projects at Interior. It was 1965 and I was getting my hopes up for that promotion to Assistant Director. But then things took a turn for the worse. There was change in the leadership at the GAO. Jim Hall, a newly promoted Assistant Director arrived in D.C. from the San Francisco office. Call it a personality conflict if you will, but unfortunately Jim and I just did not get along from day one.

One of the unwritten rules in GAO was that without prejudice everyone was entitled to request one transfer without explanation. I'm thinking now was a good time to exercise that option.

I had worked very closely in my earlier days with GAO Director Samuelson's assistants Jack Mertz and Joe Comtois. In fact, Joe and I would become close friends and served as each other's best man when we got married. I called Joe and told him I was not happy and wanted to exercise my one-time transfer. Shortly thereafter I got a call from the Director.

"When I would you be available for transfer?"

"Tomorrow would be soon enough."
"Gee John, I gather that you really want to move."

"Yes sir, as I said, tomorrow would be fine."
The following Monday, I was assigned to the powerful Senate Appropriations Committee where I spent six months helping the Agriculture subcommittee process the Department of Agriculture's huge and complex appropriations. I got a good insight into the behind-the-scenes workings of the United States Senate. That would benefit me later on.

It was toward the end of this assignment that I met my wife to be, Lorraine. We would be married the following fall.

On completion of my Senate tour, I was assigned to the Department of Commerce and shortly afterward I was promoted to Audit Manager at the GS-14 level. I replaced a manager who had issued a series of reports concerning the administration of business and urban redevelopment. His reports pertained to economic development issues, loans and grants to various organizations to create job opportunities in distressed regions and communities.

Just then the "rules of engagement" suddenly changed at the GAO. In prior years, small reports were prepared on individual investigations and issues. Now we were being asked to do more comprehensive investigations in our routine reports. The best way to describe my four-year tour at Commerce had to be unexciting. We prepared a number of audit reports on bad loans and grants and accounting issues pertaining to loan collection. However, nothing was close to what I would call "front page" material.

Too bad—Have to admit, I kinda liked the limelight.

The uneventful time at Commerce was made worse by a bad case of GAO political infighting. Assistant Director Don Pullen was a very well-liked individual who worked for an Associate Director named Henry Eschwege. For several years those two did nothing but fight and their disagreements inevitably trickled down to me and the other two Audit Managers. At one point in time, all three of us under Don Pullen were looking for jobs outside of GAO. Eschwege was aware of that and believed it was somewhat a reflection on his managerial abilities, which of course Pullen resented. Fortunately, we managed to keep busy with an ever-increasing load of Congressional requests—so the years passed quickly.

It was now June 1970 and I was again up for reassignment. As I wrote earlier, each reassignment within the GAO is critical. Each time, you hoped to be placed in a position for advancement—careers depended on it. I met with the Director again and he told me I was going to the District of Columbia audit site to do a "special project". My heart sank. I had been caught in the feud. Both Pullen and Eschwege were conservative, but at least Pullen was open occasionally to try new things. As I supported Pullen, it was clear I had been done in. It was during that period as I was considering leaving GAO for another position, when Director Samuelson called me in.

We had a heart-to-heart chat. He said some very nice things about my work and indicated that I had the potential to move to the next position. I would find out in later years he generally tended not to be very honest with people he did not plan to promote. He wanted to keep them doing a good job at their present level to help him look better at controlling costs—not to mention that few even wanted to work for him in the first place. He would just not tell the truth. Things then actually would get worse.

My special project in D.C. was to study the duplications created in the multitude of federal grant in aid programs. The Comptroller General himself had requested the study, concerned that there was much overlapping and waste.

If there wasn't, it would be the only government program without such waste.

Director Samuelson and I were to meet with the Comptroller General to get his thoughts and procedural directions on the special project. It was my first meeting with new Comptroller General Elmer Staats. He had vast experience and had been a senior official in the Bureau of the Budget and had been a budget advisor to five presidents. Unfortunately, it quickly became clear to me that Samuelson and Staats did not get along. Joseph Campbell, the former Comptroller General, had let Samuelson run his outfit the way he thought fit. Staats however appeared to have a more hands on approach, particularly with regard to directing and prioritizing various assignments. After our meeting, I thought I had a good insight into what the Comptroller General wanted. But on leaving the Comptroller General's suite, Samuelson turned to me.

"John, don't pay any attention to what he just told you, he does not understand. I will tell you what I want you to do."

Now suddenly I was in the middle, caught between Samuelson and the Comptroller General. It was not a very pleasant feeling.

I returned to the audit site which strangely enough was directly across the street from the Commerce Department where I had worked for four years. I had been assigned two new staff members, Bob Derkits and Chet Janick. We began analyzing the hundreds of federal grants received by the District of Columbia. We began to grasp the enormity of the task. Almost immediately a pattern began to unfold in several areas.

We noticed a large number of federal programs that provided for childcare services, job training, and for health care. We selected the childcare area first and proposed to do a study in this area to identify the number of programs involved and how (and if) they were coordinated. We sent audit order paperwork over to Samuelson for approval. He was out of the office on extensive travel so his deputy, Art Schoenhaut, gave us the go-ahead. Since the job was tagged "special", we also sent the paperwork up to the Comptroller General. We got a note back indicating that he liked the approach we were planning very much. Our associate director, Irv Crawford, also was on board with the Comptroller General 100 percent.

When Samuelson returned from his trip, he saw the job description and note from the Comptroller General and (no surprise) was furious. He called me immediately and yelled that if he had been here, he would not have approved the job the way I outlined it.

So, I guess I was still in the middle.

That said, the job still was different and exciting. There seemed to be plenty of waste to uncover. We were able to identify 11 federal programs providing funds for childcare services in the District of Columbia. The 11 federal programs provided about six million dollars and funded approximately 62 private and public childcare centers in the district, serving about five thousand children. There were six programs housed in the Department of Health, Education, and Welfare; four programs in the Department of Labor; and one program in the Department of Housing and Urban Development. The funds then flowed through a dozen different local agencies within the District of Columbia.

What a nightmare. We found there was absolutely no

coordination between the federal agencies and the local District of Columbia agencies. Using this information, we developed a series of comprehensive charts showing how these programs created bureaucratic layer atop bureaucratic layer.

Also, to no one's shock, we also found a very inefficient operation in the actual administration of the programs. We analyzed some of the areas where the centers were located. The primary age group targeted was three and four year olds. We were able to obtain information from the Bureau of the Census to show that some individual centers had more capacity than the entire population of three and four year-olds in the service area. Yet other areas of the city were jammed with waiting lists due to their inefficient operations. With so many players gouging for monetary turf, and with no central leadership, there was absolutely no way there *could* be an organized plan.

Then too, the way some of the programs had been created was odd. Congress had created a program called the Elementary and Secondary School Education Act. Its intent was to provide childcare for the youngest "*educationally* deprived" children. Also along came the childcare programs of the 60s and the famous Head Start program. That program was to benefit the "*economically* deprived" child. How was an educationally deprived child and an economically deprived child — supposedly different target groups — to be identified? The answer was simple. INCOME.

The conclusion was obvious because in fact, there was no difference between the target groups served by these different programs. The government bureaucrats and politicians had created another unnecessary bureaucracy. On top of all that, the HUD Model Cities program added yet another layer. I would later brief the Chairman of the House Education and Labor Committee on the conflicts. I was sure that soon everyone would be working for a

74

government paycheck—a big concern, and still much in the head-lines today.

We found some childcare centers had direct or indirect funding from all 11 of the federal programs. One of my less than brilliant ideas was to visit a local childcare center and take a picture of all the children. I would then blot out their faces and replace them with a list of all the programs under which they were covered. We concluded that might be a little too dramatic, but the charts we prepared and included in our report were still very impressive. They clearly showed how Congress had passed a multitude of laws that provided layer on top of layer of federal programs.

With expectations low, we brought our report and charts to Samuelson who was "not impressed". Lacking his support, we discussed the matter directly with our Congressional relations staff. We somehow needed to get all the damning information in front of the relevant Congressional committees—but we were stone-walled. We strongly suspected that the staff had conferred with Samuelson who of course had killed our attempted end run. Finally, Irv Crawford, our Associate Director who was as frustrated as anyone, came to my rescue and made a decision.

Every fall season each GAO Associate Director held a review meeting with the Comptroller General. It was up to the Associate Director to organize and present information pertaining to all of his audits, both underway and planned. Since he felt my report deserved attention, Crawford told me he would put me on first and would devote a major portion of the meeting to our childcare study. We went to the Comptroller General's briefing room with our charts. Samuelson did not know what was coming.

Crawford introduced me and I was on. He told Staats, "Wait 'til you see the outstanding work that can come out of Sammy's doghouse"—referring to the D.C. audit site. The briefing lasted about 20 minutes. Using the fancy overlay charts, I explained what we had found and discussed the causes of the overlapping and duplication of the federal programs. The demonstrable waste in federal dollars ran into the millions. The Comptroller General was elated and congratulated my team for our work.

On the other hand, Samuelson was angry, and I was in trouble. Comptroller General Staats asked if I had tried to get the message via the liaison staff to the Congressional committees. I said that I had talked to the Congressional relations office but they had taken no action. Since they were attending the briefing, the Comptroller General asked them for an explanation. He got a vague response and told them if they couldn't do their jobs, that he would do it for them.

Add me to one more group's enemies' list.

Comptroller General Staats moved quickly. In less than a week he called me to tell me he had made arrangements for me to personally brief several Congressional committees as well as separately, the city council of the District of Columbia. To no one's surprise, shortly thereafter I received a call from Samuelson. He again was livid. He had been notified by the Assistant Comptroller General of something which even I was not aware of—that Staats wanted me to give the same presentation to his Panel of Executive Advisors. The advisors all were nationally known individuals.

When I received a copy of the program I panicked. The list was like a Who's Who in America—business leaders and authors plus Jim Webb, the former NASA Administrator and Cyrus Vance, the former Secretary of State, just returned from the Paris peace talks—just to mention a few.

In the days preceding the meeting I didn't sleep very well. What had I gotten myself into? Would I be able to pull it off? Crawford was delighted with the agenda but spotted my consternation. He tried to calm me down with the trite old expression, "Don't be nervous John—just remember they all put their pants on the same way you do. One leg at a time."

His humor was very helpful.

The Comptroller General was quite pleased with the charts and with the outcome of the day long presentation. He decided to make me the featured speaker at the dinner they were having that evening. It was exhilarating after the briefing when the Executive Panel gave its full support to the Comptroller General's position that we had to get this message to the Congress—and fast. But unfortunately, Samuelson was at the dinner fuming and scowling over his filet mignon. I was now in even worse trouble but had no way to let the Comptroller General know. At this point, I was very frustrated. The Comptroller General thoroughly approved of my work but my Director disliked it.

What an annoying kettle of fish to be in, but the Comptroller General did prevail.

With our childcare report behind us, my audit team moved into the area of health care. Same type of findings all over again. Colossal waste of layers of federal programs on top of each other. Throughout the District, health care centers were so poorly placed that on the map they looked like randomly shaken pepper grains. Could there have been political influence in their choices of neighborhoods? Some centers were overloaded with people lined up all day long. Others totally empty, and many in a total state of disrepair.

At one point, we took a number of pictures to show the poor conditions of the health centers. They were pretty awful. I remember one in particular where the examination tables were covered with sheets because of the huge hole in the ceiling with the plaster dropping down onto the tables. The sheets would be removed to examine a patient and then replaced when the patients' examination was completed. Dirt and grime pervaded the hallways and rooms, sanitization was impossible. We filmed untended, overflowing garbage cans. Rodents were everywhere.

We briefed the city council on our findings, including Mayor Walter Washington. The Mayor was the most anxious about the slides, but not about the filthy conditions they showed. He was concerned that it might generate much "unrest" in the underserved parts of the city and asked that we not make the slides public. Politics again!

After consultation with the Comptroller General, it was agreed the slides were pretty gruesome. They really would not be necessary to prove our point to the Congress. So, we drew up yet another set of charts showing how those particular programs overlapped and duplicated each other and were poorly coordinated—and the resultant millions wasted. As explained below, Congress did take some action.

Next it was on to the job training sector. That was the most comprehensive and difficult report because there were so many programs. We followed the same template, using similar type charts showing the history and development of the programs. The job training programs were even a worse nightmare than either the childcare or health facilities. There was so much "pork" being distributed we could have had a massive bar-b-q. Just in the District of Columbia, about 23 million dollars was provided annually by 17 manpower programs with 76 local operators providing service in a completely uncoordinated fashion. The result, of course, was some classes were empty and others were overloaded.

The bottom line was the government's money was being wasted in *all* childcare, job training, and health care programs. Despite the uproar from the D.C. politicians, our extensive reports recommended, and the Congress subsequently passed, the Concentrated Employment and Training Development Act that consolidated many of these programs—saving untold taxpayer dollars.

A small but meaningful victory—but more politics to come.

A few weeks later I got a call from Assistant Director Crawford who asked for a meeting. We had worked very closely for months on these assignments and he had made several favorable comments up the ladder about my work. He also told me he wanted to get me promoted. I was excited because I knew it was about time to receive my annual efficiency rating.

He shut the door. He looked glum. He handed me the rating report. It was not a bad rating, but I knew it was not one that would move me into the ranks of my ultimate career goal of becoming an Assistant Director.

"So, Irv, what the hell happened?"

He was the most honest of any individual that I had ever worked for in GAO. He laid it on me straight.

"Samuelson has lied to you for the last couple of years. I directly submitted a perfect rating that would have easily gotten you promoted to Assistant Director. Samuelson personally reduced the rating."

In those days, one's supervisor had to review the ratings before they officially could be issued. He told Irv that if I wanted to move up career wise, his suggestion to me was to make a move (i.e. get rid of me)—either within the agency or outside. I always appreciated Irv's advice. Naturally I was terribly disappointed. I had been penalized for doing exactly what the Comptroller General wanted me to do, but in the process alienated my direct supervisor—Division Director Samuleson. I realized that these conflicts and disappointments occur in government and in the corporate world as well—but it was still a bitter pill.

Now it was 1973 and the GAO was undergoing yet another reorganization. It created a new division to be responsible for all accounting and financial management activities. My friend, Don Scantlebury was named the new Director. Don asked me to give a briefing to his senior staff on the approach we took on the audit on grant studies. I saw there might be a good opportunity. After the briefing I asked Don point blank if he had any openings. On the spot he made me an offer for a senior position in his accounting systems operations group. He said it would have the potential for advancement to Assistant Director. I jumped at the opportunity to put the Samuleson affair behind me—or so I thought. The paperwork was processed; however my actual transfer was held up for about four months. I did not understand why until I finally arrived on the scene.

Often in a reorganization, especially when a new unit is created, strange things can happen. Usually the existing unit—which just happened to be run by my nemesis Samuelson—is minimized and must give up personnel and resources. Naturally the existing units try to get rid of their worst employees. GAO was no exception. Since most of their operating level auditors had worked for me on the Treasury assignment, I knew the relative strengths and weaknesses of most of the staff. Had Scantlebury brought me on board earlier, I would have been able to stop what I called "the big toilet flush" that Samuelson pulled on the new division. As a result, he sent over the worst performers. But at least I was off to a fresh start.

8. An Early Look At The CIA

During the period from 1966 through 1970, I was in charge of GAO audits at many separate agencies in the Department of Commerce. I had been promoted to a GS-14, GAO Audit Manager. Most of our audit and investigative activity was concentrated on an agency called the Economic Development Administration — and for good reason. They provided communities large amounts of funds in the form of direct grants and loans. Their purpose was to stimulate economic development in various depressed areas of the country. It was a classic give-away program and ripe with opportunities for fraud. Many of the loans would never be repaid. When loans or grants were approved, frequently the check would be given to the local Congressman who would present it to the entity. Actions like these always play well for the Congressman, particularly at election time.

One day I took a call for what I thought was a routine Congressional request. We were being asked to investigate matters of possible double compensation pertaining to government translators working for the Joint Publications Research Service (JPRS). The Congressmen had received information that translators were receiving a full government salary and were moonlighting by doing piece translation work for other activities of the government as well. The JPRS was listed as an Agency within the Department of Commerce.

When we begin work on a new audit or investigation, we usually notify the Department's Internal Auditor and the senior official in the Department who is responsible for oversight of the agency. In recent years I had gotten to know the Commerce Department's Director of Administration very well. Don Moore and I had created an exceptional working relationship between his Department and GAO. I stopped by to see Don, to advise him I had an official request to investigate the JPRS and needed to know a contact point. He got a strange look on his face, asked me to sit down, and shut the door.

"John, they are not ours." Right then and there I knew what was coming.

Most everybody in this town refers to the CIA as the agency that nobody works for. I had guessed right. Don was now whispering. "It's not ours, it's a CIA operation." He revealed they were placed in the Commerce Department budget, but they were a totally independent operation and reported to no one at Commerce. He gave me the name of the individual purportedly "in charge".

I called the individual to make an appointment. I offered that I had been asked by certain Congressmen to investigate the use of translators by his organization. He asked if I was familiar with the functions and responsibilities of JPRS. I said I was, without ever mentioning the CIA specifically. I alluded that I also knew that the oversight of his organization would probably *not* be the same Congressional committees that oversee the Commerce Department.

We arranged to meet a few hours later. JPRS was located in an old, World War II temporary building on Washington's Great Mall. It has long since been torn down. We discussed the nature of the request and I asked for information on the policies and for access to the payroll records of several of the suspected translators. His door was closed and the two of us discussed the request in rather hushed tones. He disclosed that the many translators that were employed in this organization were unaware who their actual parent company really was. Furthermore, the parent company was not the CIA directly, but another company commonly called "a proprietary". The proprietary was a company located in Arlington, Virginia named the Foreign Broadcasting Information Service. In the meeting the gentleman never actually referred to the CIA by name, he referred obliquely to the agency once or twice by saying that he was the only one that knew who the ultimate employer was.

Then things got interesting. He pointed out that GAO had no investigative authority over the CIA. I'm sure he expected me immediately to cave, but I retorted that we were investigating a Commerce Department agency called the JPRS. That said, I indicated I understood the true situation and that we were working on that problem with the requester. Our Legislative Liaison, Marty Fitzgerald, discussed the issue with the requester — advising that this was an intelligence operation, and the requester might wish to withdraw the inquiry for that reason. But of course, the requester was adamant.

"There are too damn many sins being covered up by the excuse that it is an intelligence operation."

Now more than ever he wanted us to pursue the matter. So, our legislative liaison then decided to meet with the Armed Services Committee, the committee at that time did have the responsibility for the CIA.

In the meantime, I was informed that someone from the proprietary company would set up further discussions and a potential resolution of the problem. It didn't take long before I received a call from a Mr. Brown, obviously a pseudonym.

Arrangements were made for me to be picked up and taken to the proprietary in Arlington. The "arrangements" were something that someone would expect in a spy novel. I gave them a description of myself and was told to stand at noon tomorrow on the corner of 14th and Constitution Avenue next to the Commerce Department building and adjacent to the Washington Monument. I would be picked up and driven to the location for the meeting. It all sounded very strange and was certainly not the way GAO auditors and investigators were normally treated in dealing with federal agencies. But then again, nothing about the CIA is particularly normal.

Meanwhile, I got a call from Marty Fitzgerald. Marty told me that he had just met with the Armed Services Committee. Of course, they were well aware of the JPRS operation. They had contacted the Congressman who sent in the request to GAO and directed him to cancel it. He did. Marty said that since now we have no authority to investigate the CIA, we should do no further work. I called "Mr. Brown" back and advised him that contacts had been made through the House Armed Services Committee to withdraw the request and that at this point I saw no need for our meeting scheduled for the next day. Mr. Brown concurred and quickly terminated the conversation by asking me to destroy any reference to his name, his organization, and the phone number he had given me.

... a little spooky.

Thank goodness today the GAO does have the authority to investigate the CIA. And even though we didn't get to do our audit at the time, I certainly got a bit of an understanding how the CIA operated—as well as good insight into their considerable power on Capitol Hill. I would come again head-to-head with that power during our upcoming Iran-Contra investigation.

9. Auditing And Investigating The President Of The United States

It was the spring of 1975. I was an established Assistant Director. Lorraine and I were living relatively comfortably in Great Falls, Virginia and the boys were growing up fast. Patrick was now five and Kevin two.

But the Nation's wounds were still healing from Watergate. President Ford had taken over and was gradually moving his people in and the Nixon people out. He was a skillful politician and a good manager who did a much better job than the nation gave him credit for. I too had survived Watergate, and by now the famous tapes had been made public. I was now well aware that it was President Nixon himself that had ordered us out of the White House. Things were pretty much back to normal routine. My staff and I were working on long range plans and a couple of other unexciting audits when my secretary announced a call from Phillip Buchan, the Counsel to the President.

"Uh—oh, what now?"

My instincts sensed the situation correctly. Mr. Buchan said he had two requests: the first was that President Ford would like the General Accounting Office to come to the White House and do an audit of the books and records of the Office of the President through August 9, 1974 the date President Nixon left office. The new President wanted to start his administration with a clean slate and put the past behind him. Remembering the condition of the White House records and what we had been through in 1972, I declined to do the audit. I explained my concerns over the condition of the records and the potential of raising a number of the Watergate issues all over again. Mr. Buchan was adamant, so I suggested gently he call the Comptroller General. He ended up approving the audit as is detailed in the next chapter.

The second item he asked for our assistance on was more specific. One of the many abuses that had surfaced during the Nixon administration was the government's subsidy of the two Nixon residences at Key Biscayne, Florida and San Clemente, California. Secret Service and other funds were used to make major improvements to both residences, under the guise of protecting the President. New furnaces were installed, wind screens were put up on the swimming pool at San Clemente, lighting and alarm systems were installed, plumbing throughout was upgraded. Some weak justifications were provided when we questioned these expenses. The Secret Service maintained the swimming pool wind screen was not a wind screen but a bullet-proof shield to protect the President from attacks from vessels miles away in the Pacific; the furnace was to preclude the possibility of an explosion and fire.

The end result of these shenanigans was Congress passed a new law limiting the President to one residence outside the White House. The legislation also pertained to the Vice President. It further set forth certain rules and procedures as to how property improvements made by the Secret Service or any other government agency were to be handled.

Basically, at the end of the term in office, they had to be removed. If they were not, a value was placed on them and the President or Vice President reimbursed the taxpayers for them. The President and Vice President were afforded options as to how they wish the improvements handled. There had been limited improvements made by the Secret Service to then Vice President Ford's home in Alexandria, Virginia. Since President Ford had just recently signed this legislation as passed by the Congress, suddenly he realized he did not have the opportunity to make the upgrade elections as offered by the new statute.

To make matters worse, he now had a sales contract for his house in Alexandria and was concerned that some of the improvements the Secret Service had made would cause him a problem in selling the house. The improvements were not elaborate and consisted of living quarters that were added to his garage to provide space for the Secret Service detail on a 24 hour a day basis. At that time, the Vice President did not have a separate government-owned residence as he does today. The matter was somewhat critical because the President had a contract to sell his house that expired in three days. He wanted an answer from the General Accounting Office as to whether and how that particular provision of the statute would be handled in his case. Obviously, there was no opportunity for the Vice President to make his elections since improvements took place before the law was passed.

Legal decisions and opinions of this nature are handled by GAO's Office of General Counsel. For years the GAO had the responsibility for providing legal review and decisions regarding laws passed by Congress. I called one of the attorneys that normally handles this type of legal interpretation and explained the problem — and its urgency. I headed across town from our satellite offices to the GAO main building for a quick meeting and explained the details of the situation, and that the President needed a decision quickly. After discussing the matter with counsel, it was clear I had already identified the problem: the President did not have the opportunity to select the options in the new law at the time he was Vice President. To estimate the cost of the improvements and to request the President to pay for it retroactively did not seem fair in light of his inability to exercise his options. A quick check with the Secret Service indicated that the facilities would cost more to remove than they had been to install, if the President chose that option. The cost of removal would be a huge mitigating factor in determining the price to be paid. Along with two of my staff, we arrived at the General Counsel's office which was located on the opposite end of the Comptroller General's office suite.

We gradually started walking in that direction through the supervisory chain in the Office of General Counsel. Bureaucracy and protocol required we be intercepted by several Assistant General Counsels. Patiently as I could, I explained to each the details of the situation. We all discussed what to do but it was clear none of the alternatives were very viable or fair to the incoming President; except perhaps the alternative of doing nothing. Finally, we moved to the office of a Senior Associate General Counsel, a woman by the name of Rollie Effros.

After outlining the issue yet again, Mrs. Effros expressed concern. She recognized the difficulty of enforcing the statute on the President without his opportunity for election—in essence a retroactive penalty.

"Mr. Cronin, I think it would be best under the circumstances if you called the White House and told them we can't possibly respond to this request for a decision in a day or two in light of the research that is required."

I thought for a moment or two, and said,"Mrs. Effros, I have a better idea. Why don't *you* call the White House and tell them that we can't possibly respond to this issue in a day or two even though the President has requested it."

At that point I think she understood the predicament a little better and that it was her responsibility to resolve it. She announced that we should discuss it with the Comptroller General. As he was not available for several hours, instead we met with her boss, Milt Socolar, the General Counsel. Milt was both a lawyer and a CPA and immediately understood the sensitivity of the issue. After listening to a discussion of both sides, he concluded that we should take no action. He suggested that I tell the White House that since the President had no opportunity make the elections as Vice President, we would consider this a closed issue, look the other way, and not pursue it.

However, of course we would be unable to put that in writing. I returned to my office and called Mr. Buchan. I told him of the GAO decision. Mr. Buchan expressed some concern that there was no written record, so I offered him the opportunity to call the Comptroller General. I was informed later that he did. Although disappointed that they did not have a document of our decision, they accepted the arrangements as made.

10. Some Things Never Die—Nixon White House Audit

In the course of discussing the issue of the sale of President Ford's house, I was advised that he also had requested the aforementioned audit of the Nixon White House accounts be reopened. Based on past troubles, I reiterated my reasons for not wanting to perform such an audit. My mind was changed quickly when not only did I get a phone call from counsel to the President, Phil Buchan, but also a letter from him to the Comptroller General insisting that the audit be performed.

Since this audit was at the President's request, as opposed to the Watergate Investigation, this gave us the opportunity to establish some ground rules. I insisted we have full and complete access to the White House, all the offices and records, and the residence as well. This would require what was known as a "West Wing Access Badge." That request did not go over very well with the Secret Service and others. Never in the history of the White House had GAO auditors been given such a badge. The badges were reluctantly provided.

Guess my uncanny powers of persuasion worked again...

My staff was now built up to about 20. I had been able to gradually get rid of most of my "problem" cases and hired some good new team members, many of whom were transfers from other parts of GAO. They were aware of the more aggressive auditing we were doing and also of our accomplishments. I also hired a few from other federal agencies and CPA firms.

This time into the White House fray we were prepared. I tapped two of my top staff auditors, Jim Krawchyk and Allen Lombard, and we headed for the White House. Our first stop was the Secret Service Offices to pick up our photo ID badges. We gave them our names and filled out the paperwork. We then identified ourselves as GAO auditors.

That's when the fun began.

When the Secret Service personnel heard that, someone exclaimed there must be a mistake here. "We do not grant GAO that type of access." Amongst the flurry and fuss, the Agent in Charge and I engaged in something of a stare-down until I spoke.

"If you have any questions about this matter call the Counsel to the President."

He was out of the room for only a few moments only to return and tell the processing people to provide us the access badges. I was pleased to see another White House tradition had been broken.

Our next step was to visit the White House administration office. Wilbur Jenkins who had given us such a hard time previously was gone. I found out further that Noble Melancamp, another serious thorn in our side during the first Watergate investigation, had in reality been a Foreign Service officer recruited from the State Department. It surprised me that the Executive Assistant to the president would be a state department detailee. At any rate, Melancamp had been transferred to our embassy in Moscow—I assumed that was to keep him as far away as possible from the current administration — and me. Art Pettipas, who had been Jenkins' assistant, was now in charge. His principal assistant was Richard White, who was also present during the Watergate period.

We explained the scope of our audit and what we planned to do, including my newly negotiated ground rules. We would look at the accounting system, the payroll systems, procurement and property practices, and in general, review all the internal control structures currently in place that were supposedly to prevent abuses. The meeting was much more open and friendly than our prior visit. We reminisced a bit about the Watergate period. Art Pettipas and Dick White were very apologetic about the difficulties that they had caused us in the past and made it very clear they were only acting under orders.

They provided us with some office space and informed us that we were free to go anywhere. We could see anything that we wanted to see, with the exception of what were called the "unvouchered accounts", the confidential accounts of the President which were exempt from GAO examination by statute. Unfortunately, this basically kept us away from all expenditures for maintaining and operating the White House residence and a good portion of the expenses for the White House.

I thought — uh-oh, here we go again …

It restarted the old battle over what constituted confidential expenditures. The law was deceptively simple. It said that some White House expenditures could be expended solely under a certificate from the President and thus were not subject to GAO review. There were, however, no certificates issued by the President. All that existed to supposedly distinguish these expenditures was that rubber stamp on the vouchers that read "By the direction of the President." The routing policy for certain vouchers, such as

White House travel, was for a clerk in the administrative office to affix the stamp.

We took the position that unless the President made a clear delegation in writing or signed a certificate after the fact specifically identifying the exempted expenditures, that we had the right (and duty) to examine and investigate all such disbursements. This issue would continue for years until finally Congress enacted a special law authorizing us access to the President's confidential accounts. It didn't help that many of the questionable expenditures involving now-familiar infamous Watergate names had been replaced by "staff member" in the report. But for now, we were limited to the regular appropriation accounts.

Despite being thus hampered for the scope of the audit, we decided to run tests from the period of July 1, 1969 to the date requested by the White House, the end of the Nixon administration, August 9, 1974. What we found was a complete lack of control over procurement, property usage, and other expenditures. Many of the questionable and improper expenditures related to the Watergate period, which made the job of reporting all the more difficult due to the notorious authors. Some of the abuses we found were unsupported rentals for a conference room for Howard Hunt and a stag dinner, without explanation, which was thrown by Gordon Liddy. The small $10,000 entertainment account for White House staff members was exceeded in violation of the law. The law was called the Anti-Deficiency Act and provided a criminal penalty for violation. Another incident that caused the amount to be exceeded was a substantial Kennedy Center bar bill run up by Henry Kissinger, a member of the White House staff and Secretary of State during the period.

Control over funds was very loose at best. At one point when the White House thought they might be running out of money;

they had the CIA transfer about $34,000 dollars to pay for White House letters responding to people concerned about President Nixon's actions on the bombing of Cambodia. Numerous payroll expenditures and payments for travel were unbelievably sloppy and poorly supported, if at all. In many cases we did not find any authorizations for travel.

We then applied an audit procedure that was the standard in private industry. We obtained current paychecks and watched the corresponding payroll distributions. We wanted to be certain that if there was a plumber on the payroll, he was a real honest to goodness plumber. The process raised some eyebrows as we distributed checks to the cooks and waiters in the West Wing, the electricians and maintenance personnel, the ushers and all other personnel that had access.

Anyone with a West Wing access badge apparently could just walk in and show their friends around as long as the President was out of town. One Saturday, knowing the President was away, I decided to take advantage, and take two friends into the West Wing. Suddenly the Secret Service entered and more than politely escorted us quickly into the Vice President's office—just don't touch the red phone! Apparently, the President was on his way over to the Oval Office. It gave us quite an inside view of activities at the White House.

In reviewing the details of the $10,000 dollar expense account allowance that had been exceeded by Henry Kissinger's bar bill, we noticed several other abuses. The account itself was divided up between the senior staff, except that Bob Haldeman and John Erlickman seemed to have unlimited access to the funds. We noted that virtually every morning for several years, Erlickman and Haldeman would have breakfast, just the two of them, and charge the breakfast to official entertainment. Of course, no visitors from the outside were entertained. This was just one example of a pervading attitude of abuse toward taxpayer money.

The violation of trust at that level was particularly irritating to me. I felt something should be done beyond my mere audit reporting. I decided to take one other action, even though the amounts were relatively small—less than $1,000 dollars. I visited the Special Prosecutor whose office was still in operation since the Watergate trials were still underway. I laid out what I had found and pointed out to the special prosecutor that this amount should be considered taxable income since although not proper it was still income and was probably not reported on their individual tax returns. I asked that an income tax violation charge be brought against the two. I never found out if the special prosecutor pursued that, however I understand he did turn it over to the Internal Revenue Service. I hope they at least got the taxes that were due—plus penalties!

Other curiosities also arose. One of the oddest things that I noted while examining the payroll distribution was that there was a very large rustic box, padlocked in the basement of the White House. I asked what was in the box and was told that it was a supply of firewood for the President's fireplace. Why then was it locked? I was shocked at the answer. Employees kept stealing the President's firewood, so they had to lock it up.

When the Nixon staffers left the White House after Watergate, some of them were pretty permissive and helped themselves to everything that wasn't nailed down. It was easy to do as property accountability was virtually nonexistent. We noted as missing communications equipment, typewriters, and even some furniture.

Although our audit work was completed, we still found two difficult tasks remaining: a close-out conference with the White House staff on our findings and a decision on how and where to report the matters and abuses contained in our report. In consultation with our Director, Don Scantlebury and the Comptroller General, we agreed it would be inappropriate to place any sensationalism in the public report lest it reopen Watergate wounds. All agreed the Nation had been through enough trauma through the Watergate affair. The Presidential election was rapidly approaching, and it would be unfair to have this report come out and adversely affect President Ford, indeed, since he had requested it. Therefore, any references to or examples of individuals who were involved in Watergate would be deleted. We used the phrase "staff members" in discussions involving Howard Hunt, Gordon Liddy, or any of the other plumbers.

However, I had kept Art Pettipas and his staff advised on each and every one of our findings. We had reviewed together all the facts, details, and related numbers. A meeting with several Presidential assistants and the senior White House staff including Pettipas and the Chief Usher was arranged. My superiors Harry Kensky, my Associate Director, and Don Scantlebury, our Director would attend.

The meeting was set. By now I was used to working in the West Wing of the White House, and under some pretty adverse conditions. But for the members of the team that had not been there, to come on official business is an awesome and intimidating experience, beginning with the Marine guards at the door. A boding sense of great history hits one immediately on entering the West Wing. Recent photographs of the President at various speeches and events are displayed throughout the White House. We were escorted into a conference room that sits in between the cabinet room and the Oval Office. I noticed Kensky and Scantlebury studying every aspect of the room in awe.

I thought the conference itself went rather well. We detailed

---

every one of our findings in each of the audit areas. There was some discussion back and forth on causes and possible actions to be taken to tighten up the system. Some measures already had been taken as a result of the pre-meeting I had with Pettipas and White weeks before.

Of particular concern were the missing items of property, many of which had obviously been taken by the previous White House staff. I remember a particular objection when I noted the 58 unaccounted-for electric IBM typewriters. When a Presidential Assistant exclaimed, "That can't be right," I saw Scantlebury and Kensky freeze and my stomach tightened. Art Pettipas came to the rescue.

"Sir, we carefully examined Mr. Cronin's numbers and unfortunately those figures are correct."

That seemed to break the final impasse. The White House took decisive action. The security personnel of the military services as well as the Secret Service that supported the Presidential residences at Key Biscayne and San Clemente were investigated. We were later informed that many of the typewriters had been recovered at those locations, and from the homes of former Nixon staffers.

The meeting concluded shortly after noon. We had been asked to stay for a lunch in the White House Mess. This, of course, interested Scantlebury and Kensky, as well as myself as I had never eaten there. The "Mess" actually is an elegant dining room and is so named because it is operated by the Navy for senior White House staff. It is located at the first level of the West Wing just under the Oval Office. It is very small, seating only about 40 or 50. The food is excellent, and the decor is historic. I was somewhat embarrassed by the tourist-type nature of my two bosses, who constantly gazed around the room to see who was there. They picked up and carefully examined the Presidential seal on the china and glassware. I was really concerned that they might be souvenir hunters but thank goodness that did not happen. They seemed excited when they were given souvenir matchbooks with the seal of the President of the United States. As we left the White House, I could see the positive impression it had made on the Director.

We left the West Wing and as we walked down the driveway toward Pennsylvania Avenue, the Director looked at me and complimented me on the way the conference had been run.

"You did a good job, John. But I have just one question. Considering where you were, didn't it at least bother you to say all those things about the President of the United States and his staff?"

And I responded, "Don, if you have seen one set of books, you've seen them all. If after all these years I were to let myself become intimidated by their titles and fancy trappings, nothing would ever get accomplished."

The report was issued several months before the 1976 elections. We did not believe that it did any damage to President Ford, although there were a few references to it by Governor Carter in some of his campaign speeches.

So much for the White House/Watergate follow-up. Congress was still out for blood over our report disclosures and the Watergate disclosures as well. Legislation was reported to provide GAO more power and better access. A new law, Public Law 95-570, authorized and in fact required GAO to make periodic examinations of the President's confidential or "unvouchered" accounts. There have now been such audits of every President since — two of President Carter and two of President Reagan and one each after that.

It is a somewhat unusual law in that it requires that GAO report to Congress the fact that we have conducted an examination of the President's accounts. But it prohibits any disclosure of any contents of those accounts except for illegal and specific unauthorized transactions. It was a reasonable compromise in that it provided the President some confidentiality of expenditures and yet afforded GAO access to help avoid the abuses of the past. The White House was a little uncomfortable with the law for one set of reasons, and Congress for another. The White House believed that the President should have unlimited confidentiality in certain areas and of course Congress believed that he should have none.

11. Audit Of Presidents' Unvouchered Accounts

In retrospect, performing these audits provided a good inside look at the President of the United States, his personal habits and expenditures, as well as those of his family. The detailed records show his likes and dislikes and the entertainment preferences of the President and first family. One minor example was a reception Chip Carter gave for the Young Democrats. The fact that they invited one Young Republican was not sufficient to classify the event as official. We reversed that charge, and it was transferred to the Democratic National Committee.

It is clear why some measure of confidentiality needs to be afforded the President and his family. It is also important to protect some of the entertainment expenditures, particularly when foreign dignitaries are involved lest some minor indiscretion be revealed. It is interesting that all nations try to find out what we spend on the others so they can get some idea of their relative standing with the President. The three countries we noticed that would pay the closest detail to expenditures were: Israel, Egypt, and Japan. As a result, those were always the most difficult and complex state dinners and receptions etc. to prepare for.

The role of the GAO in this area was also rather intricate. The life of the President exists in three separate orbits: political activities as head of his party, his personal life, and of course in his position as the head of Government. The President receives free rent at the White House; however, he pays for his personal meals. When political events take place at the White House, the political party reimburses the White House for those events. When official affairs take place, such as state dinners, the Department of State or funds specifically appropriated to the President are used for those activities. Our biggest quarrel with White House officials will always be over the level of detail and the decision as to which category to place a particular event. We always had to ask for additional detail or at least a certification say, from the First Lady, if it was one of her events, as to the exact purpose of an event. In recent years, with the help of our standardized schedules, documentation is getting better. Guest lists are provided and are reviewed to determine allocations, makeup, and specific purpose of the event.

Rex Scouten was the Chief Usher for many Presidents. As such he was particularly unhappy with our presence which he considered unnecessary meddling in the affairs of the Chief Executive. Over the years, his judgment had never been questioned, but now GAO auditors were continuously asking him to document decisions he had made. Fortunately, we gradually worked out an understanding and relationships got better through the Carter and Reagan administrations.

When we weren't having entertainment issues with Scouten, we found ourselves continually engaged in debates with members of the White House Counsel's office regarding presidential travel.

This was another knotty area—particularly during the period prior to an election. Often one will read that the President took "an official trip." What that means is that the taxpayer pays for it. If the President or a senior staff member makes a political trip, the political party reimburses the White House for the cost of the travel. GAO took the position that the latter was inappropriate since the running of political transactions through White House accounts was not an authorized procedure. After several lengthy meetings, we compromised and had the staff bill political travel directly to the particular national committee.

One particularly interesting (although not very surprising) thing about working at the White House and dealing with White House staff, is that they frequently try to use the authority of the President without the President's knowledge. It is always "the President said this" or "the President said that."

There was one particularly difficult meeting with a presidential assistant concerning presidential travel. We were trying to negotiate an arrangement on how to handle the cost of a mixed political and official trip. This occurs where several locations are visited and the function at one location is official and at another location is political. The White House official at one point pounded the table.

"I discussed this with the President at length and this is the way he wants it."

I knew that was a bluff, so I looked the presidential assistant square in the eye.

"That's funny, I talked to the President just this morning and he didn't say a word to me about it."

My statement was in essence a little fib; however, it was reasonably accurate. I did talk to the President that morning. On the way to the meeting, he passed me in the hall, and I said, "Good morning, Mr. President." The bluff worked however, and we got back to discussing the issues at hand, probably with each of us knowing the other exaggerated the circumstances.

GAO relations with the White House steadily improved — that was up until September 1980. As the campaign heated up between President Carter and Ronald Reagan, concerns were building in Congress that President Carter was using the official expense accounts of the White House to support political campaign activities. Not just for himself, but expenses of the cabinet and senior administration officials were also in question.

The Comptroller General received an official request in September signed by 11 Republican members of the Senate and a separate request signed by three Republican members of the House. We were asked specifically to determine if government monies were used for trips that were political. The trips were by the President, the Vice President, and a number of the cabinet officials. We had to determine whether employees were detailed from executive branch agencies to the White House to perform political activity. This type of request would put us in a position of having to look somewhat beyond just the expenditures themselves. We needed to look at the rationale for the actual functions as performed by White House officials.

I set up a meeting for my team at the White House and we were told we would be meeting with senior White House officials. I remember taking a young lawyer from our General Counsel's office to assist in any legal questions. We were told we would meet with a Deputy Presidential assistant. When we arrived at the White House, we went to the office where the conference was scheduled and were told we go to the West Wing to meet with Mr. Carter. I immediately realized that was the President's cousin, Hugh Carter, Presidential assistant in charge of administration.

My young lawyer friend panicked a little bit thinking we were going to meet with the President. He shook all the way.

We were escorted to a medium size office. Waiting for us were Hugh Carter, some staff of the White House Counsel, and Mary Lawton, a well-known Assistant Attorney General who had been detailed to the White House, and members of her staff.

Quite an entourage!

Hugh Carter jumped to set the tone of the meeting. He felt that the purpose of our visit was totally inappropriate, and that GAO was without the authority to go beyond the books and records to inquire into the specific activities of White House staffers. Mary Lawton fired away with some very narrow interpretations of our basic statutes. I got little support from our very nervous attorney; he was totally intimidated by his surroundings and being so outnumbered. I made a personal note that he would never attend another White House meeting and I proceeded to defend our authority and position. The meeting ended abruptly with Hugh Carter refusing to give us access to records and activities of employees of the White House. This effectively blocked our ability to carry out the Congressional requests.

Having been through White House battles before, I took this one in stride and headed back across town to the Comptroller General's office. We decided we could not back down on this one considering the large number of members of Congress that were looking at us for an independent and objective investigation. That was, after all, our role under the system of checks and balances.

Fortunately, we had recently received new legislative clout to bolster our authority—subpoena power. We decided that this would be a good test. After meeting with the Comptroller General, I called Hugh Carter to inform him that I had met with the Comptroller General and that the GAO would be issuing a subpoena for the records of the President of the United States. I informed him that the action would be made public and that he and the President may wish to reconsider their position. He asked me what the status of the subpoena was.

"Hugh — it's in the typewriter and I will have it for the Comptroller General's signature in about an hour."

He promised to get back to me. I remember that it was a Friday morning, since each Friday the Comptroller General has a Congressional briefing with the staff on current matters involving the Congress. I attended the meeting and briefed the senior staff on the status of our request for access and of the subpoena message I gave Hugh Carter. About 30 minutes later, while other issues were being presented, the Comptroller General's secretary called me out of the meeting room to take a call from Hugh Carter. Our first test of our subpoena power had worked. The President did not wish to face the rigors of a subpoena and a public fight during the campaign over denying GAO access to records. We were told the records would be made available. Hugh Carter was livid. He expressed in very strong language that we were being used as "political hatchet men" for Republicans in the Congress.

Nothing like a little legislative muscle and the fear of scandal to gain some cooperation.

So now we were back in the Carter White House, although again under a somewhat strained relationship. Interesting enough, our work in the past made this job somewhat easier. The White House had listened to our recommendations over the years and took pains to issue procedures and guidelines for both White House staff as well as senior Executive Branch officials. White House staff and appointed officials had to follow specific procedures to avoid the use of taxpayers' money for political campaign purposes.

We reviewed about thirty trips taken by the President and Vice President and saw that the guidelines had been followed. Care had been taken to assure that on official trips only official matters were discussed. The GAO had long held the position that an administration can make public appearances to explain its policies and positions. Political party platforms were not discussed—and of course—no fundraisers!

However, when it came to the cabinet and subcabinet members in the Executive Branch, the rules were not so closely followed by individuals who were a little overzealous.

We looked at sixty-three trips involving speeches that were classified as official. The guidelines that had been established were not followed in eleven of the cases. In each case the speech makers had delivered an attack on the Republican Party. In one, the Secretary of HUD compared the Republican Party to the Ku Klux Klan. Other cabinet members referred to the Republicans as anti-union and anti-worker. Other abusers included the Secretary of Health and Human Services and the Director of Office Management and Budget and thus were included in our findings. When we presented the information to the White House, they reviewed it carefully. To avoid any appearance of a conflict, the appropriate funds were reimbursed by the Democratic Political Committee—thank goodness, without issue.

During this period, I needed to be in frequent contact with Hugh Carter. Before a report could be issued to the Congress, it was our policy that the agency in question could review and comment on it. In this case however, it was the President and the White House staff. Hugh Carter was frequently unhappy with some of our findings. The following instance in particular demonstrates the power and reach of the White House.

It was late one evening and I just had dropped off a draft of a section of the report for Mr. Carter to review. I called Lorraine and said I was going to stop at a shopping center to buy some new tires for our car. While I was driving to the tire store, Hugh Carter reviewed the report and, as I was later informed, some of the material caused him to "hit the ceiling." He called the White House operator and directed her to find John Cronin immediately. The White House called my residence and spoke to my wife, who explained that I would be home in about an hour after I stopped to buy some tires. Well, that does not slow down a White House operator one bit. Remember, this was before today's electronic gadgets—she only had a telephone land line to obtain the location of the tire store.

When I walked into the tire store, the manager saw me and in a loud voice shouted, "You must be John Cronin." Immediately, I got weak in the knees. I thought that something terrible had happened to one of my family members, since only my wife knew where I was stopping. I confirmed my identity to the manager.

"Sir, the White House is trying to reach you."

"Oh, shit, is that all? I thought it was something serious."

I remember leaving them in a little bit of shock with my reaction. The manager couldn't believe my attitude but quickly showed me to a telephone at the side of the store and I called the White House. The two or three sales personnel were trying to sell tires with one ear cocked in my direction. I was put right through to Hugh Carter. It was again one of those telephone conversations where I had to hold the receiver several inches away from my ear. To say the least, Mr. Carter was furious with our report. I told him that these were some very confidential matters that I could not discuss over the telephone, or for that matter in a public store. I succeeded in partially calming him down and told him that I would call him in about an hour. I finished my purchase and headed home. The tires worked just fine.

On arriving home, I called Mr. Carter back and by that time he seemed to have calmed down. I agreed to meet with him and take care of some of the language in the report. The particular offending segment that had upset Hugh Carter was, strangely enough, in the Introduction.

The report was the result of a multiple request from 11 United States Senators and three Congressmen, all Republicans, but we also had requests from some Democrats. Democrats in both the House and Senate had sent in letters, carefully worded, asking for a copy of the report. In the Introduction to the report, I had referred to the request as a demand for an investigation made by all the Congressmen. Carter was livid. He felt that the wording implied that the Democrats in the House and Senate had also asked for this investigation—which was untrue. I calmed him down by acknowledging that he was correct and that it was more of a typographical error that we used the same Introduction in all four reports. I agreed to make the necessary correction. He seemed pleased, particularly since we had given the President and the Vice President a clean bill of health and a pat on the back for trying to issue some regulations in an area where there was no definitive legal guidance.

We now turn for a moment to our first audit of the un-vouchered accounts of the Reagan administration. One of the things I disliked about any change in the administration is that after I develop a good rapport and build confidence within a particular White House administration, there is an election, there is a change, and then I have to start over building new confidences.

I was very impressed with one particular young Presidential Assistant in the Reagan administration. John F. W. Rogers was only in his late 20s and had been made a full Presidential Assistant in charge of administration. Rogers clearly wanted to do the right thing and we built up a level of trust between us very quickly. This led to a smooth audit of the 'sometimes touchy' un-vouchered accounts. Naturally Rogers wanted to know everything we had found, but unlike other administrations, he promised complete corrective action *and* lived up to his promises. Even such minor issues as sloppy and difficult-to-audit vouchers by senior White House staff and officials was something that he thought should not happen. He took action with the White House officials and made them do it right. I was truly impressed.

One of the options we gave each administration was that if something political or inappropriate had crept into the accounts because of the difficulty or complexity of decision making, we gave the White House the opportunity to consider it an "error" and allowed the replenishment of the funds.

However, one particular episode involving Presidential Assistant Michael Deaver was very troublesome and did put a strain on our relations with the White House. Many of the White House staffers are permanent in their positions, particularly the individuals in the Ushers and Accounting offices, since one needs continuity from one administration to another. After we began our audit, an employee of the White House whispered to one of my staff that we might want to pay careful attention to the controls over the wine inventory. The way it was stated, it was clear we were being told a problem existed. As any auditor is required to do under those circumstances, we expanded the scope of our normal testing in the area of the White House wine purchases and uses.

Sure enough, we saw some startling notations in the records. The longstanding procedures for ordering wine had been changed. Previously the wines were ordered by the Chief Usher after a selection was made. The wine would be delivered and placed in a storeroom and removed as needed for official functions. Michael

Deaver changed that policy and ordered all wines be from California vineyards. This was not too unusual, if not to be expected, with a President from California. However, all wine shipments were delivered to Deaver's personal office. From there the shipments would then be relocated to the storeroom where the wine was kept under lock and key to prevent pilferage such as we saw with the firewood. When the cases arrived for storage, they would frequently be short two or three bottles. The employees responsible for the wine inventory became concerned lest they be blamed. In a classic CYA move, they began making notations on the inventory records as to the shortages. We added up the shortages and realized that during a period of about a year, about $1,000 worth of wine (at least five times that in today's dollars) had been removed from the shipments by Mr. Deaver.

Senior White House officials do have a small ten-thousand-dollar annual expense allowance that is split up amongst them for official entertainment. However, they are not authorized to remove or otherwise expend sums for official presidential entertainment or for their own entertainment. With that as a backdrop, we questioned Mr. Deaver's usage of the missing wine. I brought this to the attention of John Rogers. Rogers expressed great concern and I asked him to obtain an explanation. And explain he did. On October 1, 1983, Mr. Deaver prepared for us an official memorandum. The subject was the GAO review of selected presidential expenditures for FY 1982—Wine Handling and Inventory. I think the text of the memorandum should be presented here so one could see the attitude of a Presidential Assistant toward legitimate questions raised by a GAO auditor.

"I have been advised by John Rogers, Assistant to the President for Management Administration, that in connection with the General Accounting Offices ongoing review of selected Presidential expenditures for fiscal year 1982, they have raised certain questions regarding handling practices for an inventory of wine purchased by the White House for use at official functions.

"Throughout this administration, I have participated in the selection of wines to be served at official White House functions. As a result, I often place the orders for wines and early in the administration the wines were frequently delivered to my office for examination and tasting before being forwarded to the office of the Chief Usher.

"Additionally, on several occasions I removed and maintained in my office one or more bottles on the assumption that they be used for the occasional small official luncheons the President or other senior staff members host from time to time in the West Wing of the White House. Thus, occasionally cases of wine would be lacking one or more bottles when they arrived at the office of the Chief Usher.

"More recently, for approximately the past year, wines have been delivered directly to the Chief Usher without coming through this office. When I am interested in selecting a wine for an official function, where obtaining one or more bottles for a small official luncheon in the west wing, I request the same through the office of the Chief Usher. The requested wines are delivered to my office and I understand that a notation is then made in the storeroom records. This procedure has proved to more convenient for both my office and that of the Chief Usher and as the advantage of improved recordkeeping. It is my intention to continue handling wines in this fashion."

Rogers was a very capable administrator. He knew Deaver's memorandum would not satisfy the legal requirement that such expenditures be charged to the staff representation allowance. In fact, it did not even mention it. Nor did it address that use of wine for other than official presidential functions was prohibited. I suspect that Rogers and some of the other White House personnel were, which was why they appeared to be very sensitive with this issue. Rogers indicated there was nothing more he could do. I told him that this was not a proper use of funds, and even though the amount was small, the GAO would be vulnerable to criticism if we did not report it—which was exactly what I intended to do. Rogers then suggested a meeting with Fred Fielding, the Counsel to the President, to which I agreed.

Before discussing this matter with Rogers and Fielding, I had a brief meeting with Comptroller General Staats. He decided that we should take it as high as we could in the White House and tell them that we would have to report it if corrective actions were not taken. He suggested that the meeting should include our new Director, Fred Wolf.

Fred was a refreshing newcomer to the top levels at GAO. He had been a partner at Arthur Andersen, the firm from which the incoming Comptroller General, Charles Bowsher, had worked. Fred Wolf had been known at Arthur Andersen as "the renegade partner." He did not follow the traditional conservative mode of a major CPA firm. Fred was smart, fast moving, and very aggressive. On the appointed day, Fred and I drove over to the White House. Fred, being new to the environment, told me it was my meeting and that he was merely there to observe.

The meeting took place with John Rogers, Fred Fielding, Fred Wolf, and me. It began rather strangely with a very general discussion of our audit, the nature of the audit, why it was done, and finally moved on to a gradual conversation of the problem with the wine inventory. It became clear that Counsel Fielding was totally unfamiliar with the issue. After some debate back and forth, I asked him if he had seen the Deaver memorandum. Rogers had not provided it to him and I could understand the reason for that—because of the sensitivity and close association with the President. I handed Fielding a copy of Deaver's memorandum regarding the missing wine.

His eyes got very big.

His reaction was the same as the Comptroller General's response when he had read the memorandum. The pure arrogance displayed in the memorandum was unbelievable, particularly the position that the practice would be continued even though it was clearly irregular.

After reading the memo, Fielding seemed somewhat embarrassed and wished to terminate the meeting as quickly as possible. He said he now fully understood the issues and the matter would be taken care of. He indicated that the White House accounts would be made whole and that this problem would not repeat itself. Later we were advised by John Rogers that this in fact had been done. I would have loved to have been a fly on the wall when it was discussed between Deaver and Fielding. However, our job was done, the accounts were made whole, and the matter was not included in our audit report as an illegal expenditure. We did, however, brief the House Government Operations Committee staff and the Senate Governmental Affairs Committee staff on these improprieties. We had to make it clear that even seemingly trivial violations would not go unnoticed by the GAO.

So much for views "Inside the White House." My experiences there had made me a more astute and stronger audit and investigative manager. I was now very comfortable in dealing with the President of the United States, cabinet members, and other senior officials. I found it hard to believe that only a few years earlier I was a scared kid with a knot in his stomach who would lose a night's sleep before any difficult meeting.

12. The Treasury Department Mistreats Our Nation's Heros

It was early 1973 and thank goodness Watergate was no longer much in the headlines. I had been promoted to Assistant Director, my main career goal since joining the GAO. Life was good. Lorraine and I were living in a two-bedroom apartment in Alexandria with the two boys — Patrick now two and a half and Kevin, two months. Many of our friends were already in a house but we were saving in order to build our dream house. A year earlier we had purchased two and a half acres on the Potomac River in Great Falls for an amazing price of $12,000. We had to liquidate all our savings and investments since even the salary of an Assistant Director was not that much — particularly considering my counterparts in the private sector were making about twice as much. Our builder gave us plenty of flexibility, so Lorraine and I were able to do most of the painting and staining ourselves over the weekends, saving a considerable amount. With untold joy we moved in August of 1973.

Things were even looking up for my old friend, Harold. Our disciplinary actions against him had sobered him up and he was becoming a productive employee again. Within my Financial & General Management Studies Division (FGMSD), being a newly created unit, I was still looking for what I would call my "ice breaker"—a major report to announce our arrival to the older line units. I was particularly anxious to develop a good hard-hitting audit and investigation. Call me ambitious, but my primary motivation was to point out to those other Divisions who set us up by transferring their dead wood that we were more than up to the task.

Then I recalled my earlier work from ten years prior, auditing the Treasury Department. I remembered those unclaimed bonds belonging to the World War II veterans, and how our every attempt to report the abuses was blocked. The unspoken policy in those days was if you find an error against the government, go collect it back. If you find an error in the government's favor say nothing. I thought it was time for that policy to be reexamined.

I was right. Harry Kensky, our Associate Director and my boss, was also looking for a good report to announce and promote our new unit. I met with Harry and told him that years earlier I had observed a large amount of savings bonds that World War II soldiers had purchased and that the Treasury Department kept in safe keeping for them. I told him that I remembered many of the soldiers failed to claim the bonds because they were either killed in action or otherwise had forgotten about them. Harry thought I was on to something and told me to proceed. He asked me to determine the current status and to develop a strategy to make recommendations to have the bonds returned to the veterans and their families.

It was relatively simple to track the status of the bonds. Treasury kept good records—at least in its capacity as banker. The face value of the bonds was about fifty million dollars. Since they continued to earn interest after maturity, their current value was now in excess of $100 million dollars. That was a lot of money, particularly in those days. There were over several hundred thousand individual bonds in safe keeping. Many service men had only purchased one or two bonds through a small payroll allotment plan, so probably well over 100,000 service men were involved. The bonds were being held at the Treasury Department in Washington and at a number of the regional Federal Reserve Banks.

We began our examination. The bonds usually were placed in an individual small jacket about the size of the bond along with any other pertinent paperwork. In looking at a sample of the bonds, I couldn't help getting somewhat irritated with the Department's policy of taking no action and our policy of not reporting the situation because it might be considered "a claim against the government." What particularly infuriated me was a document filed in the envelope with one soldier's bonds. It was a death notice from the 82nd Airborne Division indicating the service man had been killed in the D-Day invasion in Normandy on June 6, 1944. Later, several members of Congress would use that document to severely criticize the Treasury Department officials for their uncharitable attitude toward our nation's veterans.

The next challenge was after all these years, to figure out if there was a way to find out the current location of these individuals. This is where the free exchange of information that I had developed between GAO and agency staffs becomes invaluable. I was aware that the Veterans Administration maintained a fairly complete computerized file of former service members. They had a central Texas facility that contained the most recent address on all veterans receiving any benefits from the VA. That included a VA mortgage, or medical or educational benefits.

I carefully examined the Treasury files again and noticed that each bond had the soldiers' military serial number on it. I took a sample of about 20 names and serial numbers down the street to the Veterans Administration offices and met with one of the computer operators who had a terminal that accessed the Texas system. We entered the names and serial numbers and waited.

I had a large lump in my throat.

Within a few seconds of what seemed to me like an eternity, the computer terminal began to print out a current address for more than half of the individuals. Now all that remained was to arrange for a representative audit test.

Before proceeding, we again met the Treasury officials and explained our position. We believed that they had a responsibility to work with us and the Veterans Administration to return these bonds to the servicemen. They were obstinate and repeated their position blocking a claim against the government and furthermore, the general philosophy that they were only bankers and custodians and merely had a fiduciary relationship to the Government (as opposed to the servicemen) to take care of the bonds. They had no responsibility beyond that and would do nothing.

Fortunately, the attitude at the Veterans Administration was quite different than Treasury's. They felt *their* fiduciary obligation was to return the bonds. They even promised full cooperation. So, while the VA officials were quick to recognize the possibility for severe criticism, the Treasury Department's actions were just the opposite—they did not want to be a party to it. As we shall see, the Treasury officials with which I dealt lacked even the common sense to perceive the import of the issue.

Our process began in a fairly straightforward manner. We took a statistical sample from almost two thousand of the listed service men and forwarded the names to the Veterans Administration. Normally such GAO inter-agency correspondence on an issue like this is handled at a lower level. Much to my pleasant surprise, the Administrator at the Veterans Administration responded directly to the Comptroller General with a letter indicating they had identified almost two-thirds of the account holders that we had furnished. I was beginning to feel that I was accomplishing something worthwhile, even though in a sense it was costing the government money.

I firmly believed we all had an obligation to those servicemen and particularly to the families of those who were killed in the defense of the country. Of course, the Treasury Department still disagreed with that philosophy. Not only did we quickly meet with the Veterans Administration officials, we also visited the IRS and the Social Security Administration. Those two agencies were also helpful. They could trace people through tax records and social security records given that the social security number was also located on the servicemen's savings bonds. These agencies too, quickly saw the potential of some good public relations, or at least the potential for severe criticism if they did not support this effort. Even the usually uncooperative Internal Revenue Service provided a letter advising that they would assist.

Nothing like a bit of enlightened self-interest to expedite matters…

But then again, nothing is easy in government. We suddenly learned there was an internal GAO problem. My former division, the Civil Division, got wind of our forthcoming report and the plan we had developed. Concerned that they would be criticized for not having done anything with this problem for the past ten years, the Division found an attorney in our Office of General Counsel to try to terminate the project. He contacted our Director and said we should not proceed with this assignment because it constituted the dreaded "claim against the government." Creatively they also asserted that to make the names of these veterans public in any way would violate the veteran or the veterans widow's right to privacy.

I was absolutely furious that any individual in an organization as professional as the GAO would stoop to such subterfuge. I explained in detail my position to the Director and he thought a meeting with the Comptroller General was in order. It was quickly arranged and Elmer Staats agreed to move immediately with our report. The General Counsel attended the meeting and sheepishly admitted that the claim against the government statute did not apply—reversing his earlier "informal" opinion. Undoubtedly, the veteran or his family was entitled to this bond. In fact, the government had a responsibility to return it to the veteran or the family. So now we were back on track. But without realizing it, I was now heading for my first national television appearance.

Concerned about the GAO's relationships with the media, some months earlier the Comptroller General had created a Public Information Office. This was the 1970's and the television medium was now king of the hill. The networks had frequently informed GAO that without some advance notice and of course opportunities to obtain some film, they were unable to provide coverage on GAO reports. GAO always had very tight restrictions on releasing draft reports. They only were sent for comment to the agency officials responsible for the activities being reviewed. Even those officials were given a warning that the report was not to be released. Because of that, naturally GAO thought it inappropriate to release a draft report to the media. In fact this policy also existed because of GAO's responsibility to the Congress. It would also have been incorrect to release GAO report material in the press before it was reported to the Congress—to whom GAO reports.

Comptroller General Staats believed, however, it was time to change GAO policies and had informed members of the media that when an appropriate report came along, he would consider giving them some advance notice so they could obtain film. A key condition was they had to agree to embargo the film until the report was released to Congress. Since the Comptroller General had been made aware of the savings bond report at a discussion with the Information Office, he decided that it would be a good report to test the new policy. The next thing I knew I was summoned to a meeting at the GAO building with a producer from the "60 Minutes" television show, Mr. Barry Lando.

Oh my god, I'm going on TV!

The Comptroller General himself had provided Lando with a copy of the draft report, but under the embargo rule. Lando and I returned to my office near the Treasury Department and we discussed the report. He had a lot of questions. He wondered if he could talk to some of the people at Treasury and I agreed to make the arrangements for him. I warned him of the position that the Treasury officials would take, that they had no responsibility to these service men, even though they were killed in action. That they felt theirs was only a fiduciary role and it was up to those soldiers or their widows to come to the Treasury Department rather than the other way around. Lando expressed total disbelief that anyone would take that position.

I went ahead and arranged for a meeting with representatives from the Office of the Treasurer and the Bureau of Public Debt. John Hingten was the Commissioner — an individual who I knew was somewhat anti-GAO. Lando returned from the meeting with a look of complete disbelief on his face.

"Well, what did I tell you?"

Lando was shaking. All he could do was stutter as he fumed. He mumbled several times, "I don't believe it, I just don't believe it!"

"They actually said what you said they would say, and I didn't believe it then and I'm almost not believing that's what I heard. I only wish I had the cameras with me."

I had to chuckle to myself a little bit, because I had seen the Commissioner of the Public Debt in action on several prior occasions and I just knew he would stick his foot in his mouth.

Unfortunately, in the subsequent discussions between the *60 Minutes* producers and our information office, an acceptable arrangement for the full release of the report and the TV program could not be worked out. Without skipping a beat, our information office simply moved on to the next interested party, ABC World News Tonight. Suddenly, I was meeting with another reporter, Lem Tucker.

One of the few black television reporters in the industry at that time, Lem was very hard working, intelligent, interesting, and devoted to his craft. We gave him the draft report, after which he immediately requested a meeting with the Comptroller General. He explained to us how and when he would do the story. The Comptroller General told him to deal with me as the GAO representative and instructed me to provide full cooperation.

"Now this was getting interesting…"

I was excited. Not only was here an opportunity to be involved in a major policy change for GAO but also the chance to participate in a national TV news show and see from the inner workings of how a story and a newscast are put together.

It was a scorching hot day on the first of August in 1973 but Lem Tucker was a man on a mission. He had decided to film in five locations in Washington in one day and several locations in New York City the following day. First, I arranged a meeting with the Treasury officials. Treasury realized the damage the Commissioner of Public Debt could do, so an undersecretary met with us and the Commissioner was excluded. It was obvious Treasury was very unhappy with the press having this information. In the meeting they reluctantly acknowledged the facts but were very cautious on promising any corrective action or making any "controversial" statements as the Public Debt Commissioner had.

After the meeting, Tucker filmed a wrap up on the front steps of the Treasury building, which was somewhat critical of the department. Then, it was just a short walk across the park, from the Treasury Department to the Veterans Administration.

The VA officials were most helpful and welcomed Lem and his crew. They saw an opportunity for some good coverage for themselves and their desire to help the veterans. They answered all Lem's questions and even showed how their computerized system helped track the veterans. Much film was shot. Then it was four sweaty blocks over to the headquarters of the American Legion.

The National Commander of the American Legion had his film segment shot in the lobby of their building, directly in front of a large mural of a soldier dying on the battlefield.

"Nice touch I thought."

The Commander issued a damaging statement about the Treasury official's unwillingness to take action to return the bonds to the servicemen. Then, it was off to the United States Soldiers Home.

Located in Northwest Washington, the Home catered to elderly retired and disabled soldiers that had frankly nowhere else to go. We had located one of the bond holders living there. A very ill, very old soldier. I remember how skillfully the filming was used to tell the story and demonstrate the problem. Lem was positioned on a park bench in the quadrangle of the Home and the disabled veteran was brought out to him in a wheelchair. He interviewed the veteran who thanked everybody for finding his bonds because he did not have much money. Lots more filming.

By this time, I was exhausted, but Lem was still energized—he knew this was going to be a big story. Four locations so far, and it was approaching 6 o'clock. We just made it to the General Accounting Office building to film an interview with Comptroller General Staats. He was very eloquent and supportive of the report. It was clear to him the need for the Treasury Department to take action. That over, we headed to Union Station and took the night train to New York.

The hours on the train passed quickly, having a fascinating discussion with Lem Tucker. He candidly described many details of the TV business and the challenges to blacks moving into top spots. We got to know each other quite well. By the time I got to my hotel in New York, it was nearly midnight. Exhausted, I fell asleep quickly, but with the excitement of it all; woke at the crack of dawn. We taxied to the GAO regional office in the Federal Building downtown.

Damn Manhattan traffic was much worse than I remembered.

I demonstrated to our New York GAO staff and Tucker how we located the veterans. I had shipped some computer printouts to the New York GAO office. Here was the information on the veterans that VA had located — some with addresses in the New York area. I went through the phone books and located three of them. A few quick telephone calls later and appointments were set up.

One of retirees lived not too far away in Queens. His last name was O'Connor. I will never forget it. There it was, a row house in Queens and a gentlemen with a heavy New Yawk accent. It had to be Archie Bunker's twin. Complete with the accent, he detailed how he remembered buying the bonds but didn't quite know how to get them returned. He even offered some highly critical Archie Bunker type statements about "them meatheads" in the government. It was my few minutes in the sun, literally and figuratively, because I did the actual interviewing of Mr. O'Connor. That particular day, the temperature was in the high 90s and the TV crew even added lights to properly light up the porch which, of course, made the situation more unbearable.

The next morning, I stopped by the TV studios and was permitted into the editing booth. The producer was very pleased. There was plenty of footage and it was really good stuff. Nevertheless, I needed to review the raw film to see if there was anything in it that might be illegal or objectionable. Everyone was most cooperative, and I pointed out a couple of minor problems which they agreed would not be shown. In all we must have shot a total of about 45 minutes worth of film that was then edited down to several minutes for the TV newscast.

Nothing like a little media pressure…

Things worked well after that. The report was issued in August and one or two days later the story aired on ABC World News Tonight. Shortly thereafter, other media picked up the story, including an article in Parade Magazine, which even gave the address of the Bureau of Public Debt where people could write directly and obtain information on their bonds. A senior GAO official even called me to see if there were any bonds belonging to his father. I told him all we needed was his Service Number or Social Security Number.

But, no good deed goes unpunished.

The best way to describe the reaction of the reports at the Treasury Department was "the shit really hit the fan." Additionally, a large contingent of Congressmen were upset, particularly those involved in veterans affairs Committees and projects. Treasury was clearly in for a rough time. The Commissioner of the Public Debt received nearly 100 thousand letters inquiring about the bonds.

We arranged to have a meeting with officials at Treasury—what I thought would be a peace-making meeting—and to explore possible actions available to return the bonds. I walked into the

Commissioner's office and when he saw me, it was anything but peaceful. As we had already experienced, the Commissioner had quite a temper.

"You son of a bitch, look what you did to me."

He then grabbed a handful of 50 to 100 of the letters and threw them in my face. Scattered all over the floor, I noticed many of the letters even contained the form for redeeming the savings bonds which we had published in the back of the report. It certainly was not exactly "a peace-making meeting" but the Commissioner was now forced to discuss the easiest way for him to handle the applications from the veterans — along with the promised cooperation from the Veterans Administration and the various Federal Reserve Banks.

It was pretty obvious that Commissioner Hintgen was very unhappy. Worse, he was not changing his underlying attitude toward a voluntary return of the bonds. John Carlock, the fiscal Assistant Secretary of the Treasury, was very outspoken and had joined with Hintgen in the opposition to the GAO report and particularly to the TV appearance. Without checking with me or any other GAO official, they presumed I had leaked the report. In an underhanded move, meant to disparage my work, they sent a letter directly to the Comptroller General accusing me of leaking the report for personal publicity. I was not aware of the letter until after the Comptroller General responded. He told the Treasury Department that he had made the decision in the interest of working with the press and carrying out his responsibilities to the public. While his response saved my ass, it did not help our relations with the Treasury Department.

Almost a year went by and there was no action on the part of the Treasury Department. Maybe they thought the issue would go away if they ignored it. They were wrong. One day we received inquiries from several members of Congress for GAO as to the follow up. We "advised" them that little action had in fact taken place. That did it! The House Government Operations Committee called for a full congressional hearing. Don Scantlebury and I were to be the first witnesses. At a briefing prior to the hearing, we had supplied the committee members with many of the documents that we had obtained during the audit. One of those documents was the death certificate for the soldier that was killed on June 6, 1944.

In our opening remarks, we gave a brief summary of the entire report. I remember specifically one Congressman asking me about the document from the file. When I explained the document and the date of death, he shouted, "Wasn't that D-Day?" I said yes. That was it. The Congressman went on a fifteen-minute tirade about the insensitivity of the Treasury Department officials. Then he asked me who was responsible.

Since they were next up as witnesses, precisely those responsible Treasury officials, including Hintgen, were sitting in the front row behind the witness table facing the Committee. I turned in my seat and pointed to them. It felt like I was looking into the eyes of a lynch mob.

We finally completed our testimony and Treasury was up next. The best way to describe their twenty-five minutes at the witness table would be brutal. One member of the committee even severely criticized their lack of patriotism and support for our country's heroes. It got to the point where they could not get a defensive word in edgewise. One thing was definite. They had a loud and clear mission and mandate from the Congress—get the money out to those deserving it—or else! I guess one could say the hearing had accomplished its intended purpose.

Properly chastised, they returned to Treasury and immediately began working with the Veterans Administration and the Federal Reserve Banks. I understand that most of the bonds now have been returned, however if any still remain, that is too many.

Those individuals reading this book, particularly if they had relatives in World War II, should pay attention to souvenirs and belongings and records for any reference to a savings bond or what appears to be a war bond receipt. If they can identify the existence of such a bond or even if not sure, they can write or go online to the Bureau of the Public Debt so long as they have the serviceman's name, military service number, or social security number. I doubt this chapter of my book will sit well with the Treasury Department who believes this issue was probably put to rest a long time ago.

13. The Federal Housing Scandals

If you asked your average U.S. taxpayer to identify the most mismanaged agency in the federal government, you likely would get several answers. Some would say the IRS or the Health and Welfare agencies. Others would say the General Services Administration who does all the purchasing and contracting for the federal government. Most of those people would base their conclusion on the recurring frauds that are disclosed in the news in those areas. In actuality, frauds are seldom caused by senior or even mid-level management of a department. Usually, a few corrupt federal employees are identified in these frauds. Often these embarrassing scandals reflect unfairly on the supervisors or the entire department itself.

As this chapter will describe, my candidate for the worst agency in the federal government is the Department of Housing and Urban Development. The next pages will provide ample support for my conclusion and also illustrate the point in which my career was weakened a bit when an irate Secretary of Housing and Urban Development, Patricia Harris, personally attacked me and called the Comptroller General asking to have me fired.

It was early 1975. We had moved our primary offices a block

away from the main Treasury Building. Our staff had expanded so much that we now had an entire floor of a building located between 13th and 14th street on G Street. A young man from our Cincinnati office, Dan McCafferty, had made an appointment to see me. At this stage in my career I was becoming a well-known Assistant Director reporting to Associate Director, Harry Kensky. Harry had developed great confidence in me, particularly after the coverage we received from the savings bond examination and report.

The rapid expansion of the GAO was not without some growing pains. We began to have some jurisdictional problems of possessiveness amongst the other GAO divisions. This was particularly true of those that were responsible for reviewing the programs in the various federal agency departments. In an organization like the GAO, there are inevitably overlapping jurisdictions and staffs. Some staff members who had good contacts on the hill would sometimes "pre-sell" a project with a draft letter to help assure the request gets to the proper requesting division. On occasion, that action would backfire.

My duties mostly were functional, but I did have responsibility for all accounting and financial issues in all civil agencies of the federal government. It was a big job in that it basically included everything in the U.S. Government except the Department of Defense. Over the course of my career, the GAO had developed a number of different management objectives or focal points. During these years, the objectives were all called "issue areas." Our Community and Economic Development Division was generally responsible for the issue areas involving food, housing, and energy. Its new Director, Henry Eschwege, stressed to his people that work should only be done within the restrictive program issue areas.

Now Dan McCafferty, one of our young, bright field audit managers, was sitting in my office. Dan explained to me that they had done some research at the local HUD field office in Cincinnati and had identified some potential problems. They had proposed a study of the Housing and Urban Development to Eschwage's division. The examination was aimed at looking at how the department paid or, in this case, did not pay taxes on properties they had acquired in default. Since the job seemed more of an accounting job, it was vetoed by Director Eschwege. That veto disappointed McCafferty and his Cincinnati staff, so they had come to town to try to market the job to my group.

Dan and I hit it off right away. It was the beginning of a long and lasting work and personal relationship. Dan spelled out the details to me of what they had found so far. Unfortunately, home buyers with federal housing administration (FHA) mortgages frequently defaulted on their mortgages. When this happens, HUD becomes the owner of the property. Of course, it is their responsibility to pay the local property taxes until the property is sold, usually at an auction. At the time, HUD owned about 80,000 single family properties acquired through default. They were paying taxes in excess of 25 million dollars to 6,000 taxing authorities. The problem was Dan said they had found numerous cases where the Department had paid taxes on properties it no longer owned and didn't pay taxes on ones they did own. To understate, HUD had a very sloppy system for processing tax payments.

A key piece of required GAO paperwork in those days was called a Form 100. It was the official authorization for a headquarters office and field divisions to begin an assignment. After approval by an Assistant Director, it would be approved by an Associate Director and the Division Director and the assignment could begin. In our case things went smoothly; both Kensky, the Associate

Director, and Scantlebury, our Director had enough confidence in me to approve quickly the jobs I sent over.

McCaffery had already carefully prepared the forms to justify the audit. I had to review the paperwork and retype the first page to change it to a financial and general management studies assignment, in order to prevent it from going to Eschwege's division. Dan signed it as the Audit Manager and I signed right on the spot as the Assistant Director.

Dan flew back to Cincinnati and by the close of business the next day I phoned and told him the assignment had been approved by Director Scantelbury. Dan was thrilled but seemed quite surprised by the lack of bureaucracy in our division. I told him we were new and fast moving and were trying to avoid bureaucratic entanglements that were unfortunately occurring regularly in some of the other divisions.

The very next week I visited the Cincinnati office to meet with their Regional Manager, Bob Hanlon and McCaffery plus the two Audit Supervisors who would be responsible for a lot of the detail work, Harry Sanford and Tom Bachman. We made a formidable team. Our close relationship also would result in a series of about 10 reports to the Congress on the various bungling within the Department of Housing and Urban Development. These resulted in half a dozen Congressional hearings into these activities. Besides Cincinnati, we had arranged to include our San Francisco and Detroit field offices in the study. They were included primarily because they had a large number of defaulted single-family properties.

If the procedures and activities we found in the three HUD regional offices were found in a private organization, most of the people would be fired. In the worst example, we found that HUD would continue to pay the property taxes on properties they had

132

acquired but since sold. Obviously, the new purchaser was paying nothing to the taxing authority if the government was paying his property taxes for him. On other properties, HUD would often not pay the taxes at all. Unbelievably, we found that when clerks got behind in their work, they simply would throw the tax bills in the trash. Harry Sanford actually fished some of those bills out of the trash. We verified them to be legitimate bills for houses owned by HUD. Those tax bills would come in handy as exhibits in future Congressional hearings.

Not quite so hard to believe was that the majority of the time, HUD paid the taxes late and of course was hit with large penalty and interest costs. Many times after they made the late payments, they would receive a second bill with a penalty. They then would pay both bills. Often when HUD sold a property it would "gift" the new owner the property tax for the period of time that it had held the property. In many cases the new owners failed to turn that money over to the tax authority, claiming the taxing authority would have to get it from HUD. When that bill was sent to HUD, HUD also would trash it.

What a disaster...

With all these conditions carefully documented, we opened up discussions with Joseph Luman, the Staff Director of the Subcommittee on Manpower and Housing of the Committee of Government Operations in the House of Representatives. Luman was a dynamic staff director who felt it was his personal mission to constantly pound on HUD to improve their management operations. When we presented to him what we had found, it didn't take him long to arrange for a hearing.

It was interesting how our dialogue with Luman developed. The staff within the Resources Community and Economic Development (RECD) Division was very disappointed that Director

Eschwege had chosen not to pursue the job they had proposed to expose the HUD abuses. However, they were unaware that Mc-Caffery had gone to see me and I had approved the job under our division's leadership. Some of the RCED staff members leaked some information to one of Luman's staff in the hopes they would yet be able to generate a request.

When GAO receives requests from committee chairmen, in accordance with GAO's enabling statute, we are obligated to conduct a review. The letter was prepared and sent to GAO. The RCED audit staff was delighted, thinking that they would be able to do the job. It turned the tables on them when the letter came into GAO and a simple check by our Office of Congressional Relations found out my team already had taken up the job. The letter was sent to us with the request to turn the job into a Congressional assignment which really backfired on the RCED staff.

I enjoyed Joe Luman and we would work well together for many years to come—that was until Joe later fell victim to the politics of Capitol Hill.

Perhaps I also should have been more vigilant…

The hearings began on September 25, 1975 and the Chairman along with a Congressman named Randall just plain "blasted the hell" out of the HUD officials for their negligence. He even waved the tax bills around that had not been paid that Harry Sanford had fished out of the trash basket at the department's Cincinnati office.

Where there's smoke…

14. HUD Disasters Continue

We weren't done yet. Earlier in the year we had also begun looking at HUD's payroll system. This of course was squarely within our accounting purview. We had heard through the grapevine that there were many employee complaints. Turned out it was just a really bad system. I borrowed one of our division's computer experts, Earnst Stockel, to assist some of my staff in doing some basic research into HUD's accounting methodology. We discovered it did some really strange things to the HUD employees. One example was when we talked to an employee who lived in the Washington area. She had gotten married and tried to change her health insurance from single to married. Instead of a revision in the health insurance premium deduction, the payroll department began to take out City of Philadelphia payroll taxes. It took her months and months of letter writing to get the system straightened out. In some other cases, employees simply did not receive a paycheck at all. They would be dropped entirely from the system without explanation.

When we test systems for weaknesses, we usually meet with the appropriate department officials and try to work together to straighten out the bugs. HUD of course was notorious in resisting any advice from us, so often we would have to prove things to them the hard way. We decided to run what was called a "test deck" through the HUD payroll system. The deck checked all computerized systems for a fixed number of checks. This prevented unauthorized transactions from entering. Also, things like limit checks were used to make sure that salaries above a certain amount are not paid, as well as check trials to verify social security numbers. Other verifications were used to make sure that proper cost centers and appropriations were charged—and so on.

For our friends at HUD, we devised a special test deck like none other ever used. We created 30 imaginary employees and made every conceivable records and operating error we could think of. For example, we hired one employee before he was born. We paid a number of employees a $99,000 a year salary, more than twice the legal amount of the maximum federal salary at that time. We used social security numbers from blocks of numbers that had yet to be issued. We charged many salaries to nonexistent appropriation codes and to offices that did not exist within HUD.

The *coup de grace* and the one thing we did that came back to haunt me was some of the names we chose for those employees. Understand that the computer wasn't particularly interested in a name. It controlled things by social security numbers. For our own lighthearted amusement, we decided to use some Walt Disney and other famous cartoon character names. We inputted the names Donald Duck, Porky Pig, Loony Tune, Dick Tracy, Mickey Mouse, Minney Mouse, etc. To our dismay, but not necessarily surprise, every one of the transactions processed cleanly. Then we wrote a report in June of 1975 to HUD suggesting strongly they ought to improve their pay systems. As they frequently would do with GAO reports, they promised corrective actions—maybe in the next decade.

While all this was going on, McCaffery and the Cincinnati staff completed work on another assignment. They began reviewing conditions and procedures in other HUD programs within their local office. My staff was also conducting parallel observations in Washington. Most of HUD's financial activities took place on the third floor of their headquarters in Washington. Our not so funny inside joke was that we were gradually working our way from one end of the third floor to the other and there was a management deficiency finding on virtually every desk. Our HUD efforts would last approximately five years—but what a ride.

My team also looked at the HUD system for collecting FHA mortgage insurance premiums which at that time amounted to just under $800 million a year. We found the same sloppy activities that we found with the people responsible for the tax payments. No one was watching the store in collecting the vast amounts of receivables due the government. We calculated that delinquent insurance premiums each month were about 38 million dollars. Amazingly, HUD rarely sent delinquency notices out. They just waited until the mortgage bankers they had subcontracted got around to sending HUD the funds due—if ever.

In one particularly egregious case, a major national mortgage banker, the Cameron Brown Company, had been sitting on several months of mortgage payments. That one company was holding about 1.6 million dollars in mortgage premiums due to HUD. When we made this public, there was yet another Congressional hearing. More promises to improve from the Department. At the hearing Cameron Brown Company announced that it was deeply embarrassed. They said they had prepared the checks; they just had put them in a drawer and forgot to mail them. If the reader of this book believes that and would care to contact me, I have some liquid land in Florida I would like to sell him to go with his bridge in Brooklyn.

As if all these shenanigans were not enough, we found an interesting scheme being played on HUD by the entire mortgage banking industry. Since the purpose of the program is to provide low and moderate income individuals with the opportunity to own a home, the legislation allowed for no prepayment of the first year's insurance premiums as was required with commercial mortgages. In HUD programs, the homeowner simply pays the insurance each month along with his mortgage when due. For some reason, perhaps as compensation for their processing services, HUD allowed the mortgage banking industry to retain the payments for 12 months. Obviously, they had the use of those funds. We made a recommendation that the mortgage bankers pay the amounts it was withholding in its escrow accounts immediately. On a nationwide basis it amounted to about 375 million dollars.

One of the more pervasive problems in our government that I previously referred to is that often-appointed officials come directly from the industry they are expected to regulate. This especially was true in HUD. A number of the officials there came from or were directly associated with the mortgage banking industry. Somehow, they forgot they were supposed to now be representing the U.S. taxpayers, so naturally when the industry heard of our disclosures, they ramped up their lobbying campaign. They were successful within HUD which didn't seem to care. Luckily, they were not so successful with the Congress's Government Operations Committee.

Joe Luman arranged for yet another hearing highly critical of HUD. On the Hill we testified extensively on our findings. We even testified again about HUD's failed computer systems. HUD's computer designers left a lot to be desired. As I mentioned earlier, even those early computer systems had special programs to prevent and detect errors. In particular HUD's computer system had some good edit routines expected to prevent erroneous billings. There was a limit at the time of FHA mortgage insurance of 50 thousand dollars, so the computer had been instructed to not accept a mortgage in excess of 50 thousand dollars. It had a secondary edit to be sure that on the monthly billing cycle, no bill even was sent out on a mortgage in excess of that amount.

Pretty basic stuff one would think…

While our review was going on, the Congress did raise the limit to $64 thousand. HUD dutifully changed the front edit so that the computer system could accept the $64 thousand mortgages. Unfortunately, its computer programmers "forgot" about the other edit. *The result*—the computer discarded every invoice for mortgages between 50 thousand dollars and 64 thousand dollars. This went on for a period of nine months until we discovered it and brought it their attention. The computer people at HUD did not care for us very much.

At the hearing, the HUD officials took another beating. They really didn't like GAO in general and they disliked me even more. In our testimony we talked about the earnings the mortgage banking industry received from the millions of taxpayer dollars in insurance premiums they were holding. HUD officials actually tried to take the position that those monies were in non-interest-bearing escrow accounts and so no one made any money.

One Congressman, Caldwell Butler, understandably was having a great deal of difficulty believing *any* of HUD's testimony. He realized that we were the experts, and he was not—so one day he asked us to stay after our testimony was finished, just in the event that there were any follow-up questions. He left the hearing podium and came down to the audience to where I was sitting with Don Scantlebury. Congressman Butler had a booming voice. He asked what I felt about the laughable position that they didn't earn any money on the accounts. Most of the people in the hearing room could hear our conversation. To end it quickly, I quietly whispered to the Congressman that the position was "bull shit."

"Bull shit—that's exactly what I thought they were giving me," he thundered.

The HUD officials winced. The Congressman returned to the podium and when his turn came up again, Butler announced that after he had conferred with the GAO representatives it was clear that the monies do earn interest and furthermore that he was not accepting HUD's position—period. At that, the HUD officials practically leapt from their seats scowling at Scantlebury and me. It was a look I had seen before from them. It was like looking into the eyes of a lynch mob.

After the hearing, we were asked to come to a meeting at Congressman Butler's offices. He was all too aware that even after having been chastised, HUD probably would not take action. We gave him some additional ammo and he immediately began drafting legislation requiring HUD to implement our recommendations to collect the money. Given their powerful lobbyists, HUD never expected the legislation to go through, but they mobilized anyway to try to stop it—but they were too late.

Butler had worked fast. It turned out there were some housing amendments already under discussion on the floor of the House of Representatives. Butler quickly tacked on his amendment and it sailed through. It was one of the few cases in history where a GAO recommendation was made into a legislative mandate from the Congress. Obviously, we were delighted with his actions. He was one of the few Congressmen at the time committed to improving financial management in the federal government.

With several more investigations and reports to the Congress, the hearings on HUD continued. These investigations would involve HUD's rehabilitation loan program, their multi-family mortgage insurance program, and their home improvement loan program. We found in all these programs a continuing pattern of operations highly vulnerable to fraud, waste, and abuse. Hence my opinion that HUD was the most poorly run part of the Government. We would continue these examinations until about 1981 when other areas became a higher priority for the GAO.

Many of the statistics of HUD's fraud and negligence were close to unbelievable. In the Rehabilitation Loan program alone, *53 percent* of the loans due were delinquent, with no serious attempt to collect. While some were legitimately delinquent, in many cases HUD seemed to have just lost the loan records from their systems. In the Multi-family Mortgage program, the situation was actually worse. Again, when an insured multi-family project would default, HUD would take over the project and then contract with a private company to manage the project for them. This program was riddled with favoritism and fraud and included repeated cases of diversion of funds for personal use. Just one case in New York City involved over $2 million in misappropriated taxpayer funds. Some aspects of it were personally very disheartening for me.

It was 1975 and the project was called the Delano Village Apartments in New York City, located at 139th Street and Lenox Avenue. Quickly after beginning our investigation, we realized that transportation in and out of that area for our staff was very difficult. The neighborhood was so bad that taxi cabs would not accept a telephone request, so our staff had to use a government car. When the government motor pool dispatcher discovered the employee destination, they always gave us the car with the most dents and damage that they had in their inventory. One car was so badly damaged that we could not even get the trunk open to put our briefcases and supplies inside. We thought the motor pool was just giving their good friends at GAO a hard time. But when we inquired, they said there is no sense sending a newer car into that area—it would come back vandalized—if it came back at all.

Our "first pass" analysis of the Delano project's financial statements easily indicated that "diversions" were taking place. Diversion is a polite term for stealing by skimming funds out of the venture while at the same time the project is failing to pay the government on the mortgage. The laws creating the housing programs provide for fines and jail terms for this criminal activity. We spotted some of the diversions in a footnote to the balance sheet by the company's auditor. Apparently, they had stripped out all the cash and set it up as a receivable on their books as though from a wholly owned subsidiary. The cash was then used to finance an entirely separate shopping center owned by the same management company. Immediately we had HUD arrange for a meeting at the project site to review the theft.

Obviously concerned about the possibility of criminal charges, the management company hired the prestigious Washington-based law firm, Fried, Frank, Harris, Schriver, and Kappleman—of course known as "Fried Frank" for short. Their lawyer came over to my Washington office to discuss the meeting which naturally they were trying to avoid. I insisted on it and it was scheduled for the next week. The morning of the meeting our team flew to New York on the shuttle, where we were met by our New York staff. The Fried Frank attorney flew up on the same plane with us and headed straight for the management company. A senior official from HUD's New York office also asked to attend the meeting which seemed like a promising development.

One of the tactics we had been informed the management company would take was that HUD had authorized them to use the money for other projects and not pay the mortgage.

Yeah—right!

Dan McCafferey and I and two of our top New York staff, Sam Piscatell and Ray Griffin attended the meeting along with the representatives from the company and the HUD official. It was good seeing Ray Griffin again. It was a small world since 30 years earlier, Ray and I attended Xavier High School in New York City together. We would often discuss the strange coincidence of finishing our GAO careers working together.

I began the meeting by explaining our analysis process of the project's financial statements—and discussed the diversion. We told the company official that our report would be taking the position that this was clearly an unlawful diversion of funds due the government. Just as we expected, the management company official strongly objected, stating that he had specifically discussed these activities with HUD, and an official of the Department had approved the use of these funds on another of their development projects.

"And what was the name of the individual?" I asked.

The official refused to say, and I asked, "Why?"

"They'll cut his balls off at HUD."

Up until this point, there had not been a peep from the lawyer from Fried Frank. I turned to him and said, "I think you should advise your client as to his responsibilities to answer a question put to him by a federal investigator."

The lawyer told him he did not have to respond that day but sooner or later he would be required to respond to the question in person or in writing. That did the trick, he named the HUD official—the very HUD official attending the meeting. Not surprisingly, he jumped up and in a loud voice pounded the table, glaring at me and shouted, "That's a damn lie."

That statement broke open the dike. The management official caved and started detailing all of his concerns about mismanagement in the local HUD office and in return the HUD official countered by detailing all his concerns about the mismanagement of the company.

Quite a spectacle to witness ... too bad we didn't have a tape recorder running.

However, Piscatell and McCafferty were writing as fast as they could. The attorney just kept staring at the ceiling, occasionally trying to interrupt and trying to stop the disclosures. We came out of that meeting with a gold mine of material for our Congressional hearing to follow.

Elated, we returned to Washington and prepared a formal letter to the Justice Department requesting that the United States attorney bring charges against the management officials for the illegal diversion of funds. The amount was now approaching three million dollars. Several months dragged by. Finally, I got a telegram from the U.S. Attorney's office in New York—it was a huge disappointment. Apparently in the 1970's there was very little interest in prosecuting white collar crime.

"We are not proceeding with an indictment. We feel the accounting matter is too complex to present to a jury, making conviction highly unlikely."

The experience left a bad taste in my mouth for the U.S. Attorney's office. At that time, as is the case now, a position as U.S. attorney was often a stepping-stone into the political environment. Many of the attorneys were more interested in making a name for themselves pursuing more highly visible cases involving drugs, bank robbery, kidnaping, or espionage that might catapult them into the national political scene. It was clear that a case involving the theft of a mere three million in taxpayer dollars through some creative accounting techniques just would not boost their egos enough. Fortunately, we found there would be changes in the attitude toward white collar crime in the years to come.

As disappointing as the inaction of the U.S. Attorney was, a bigger one was yet ahead. I remember the date well. It happened on October 26, 1978. Several weeks prior to that date, the GAO was contacted by the House Post Office and Civil Service Committee — Congresswoman Gladice Spellman`s Subcommittee on Compensation and Employee Benefits. They apparently had been conducting a series of investigations into several federal agencies' payroll controls with particular focus on the accounting for overtime.

We were asked to come before the Committees and brief them on our work in this area. There were two of our GAO divisions involved, Federal Personnel and Compensation Division for Personnel Matters and my division relating to the accounting matters. Hyman Krieger, director of the FPCD division, was tagged to be the primary witness and I was to support him with testimony on accounting and internal control systems.

During our meetings with the subcommittee staff prior to the hearing, I explained our in-depth knowledge on the lack of internal controls in many of the federal agency accounting systems all across the board, especially in payroll systems. I was prepared to testify on HUD, the Defense Department, and other agencies who were particularly tardy in sending their accounting systems to GAO for approval. Such approval was required by a 1950 law passed by the Congress. Most federal agencies simply had ignored the law.

In the course of the briefings, I got into some detail about our 1975 report on HUD's disastrous payroll system, and how we were able to input the 30 fictitious characters. I came prepared with the documentation and showed them some examples of the personnel documents the HUD's automated system had printed out. Ignoring the abuses, obviously they zeroed right in on the names. They saw Donald Duck, Porky Pig, Mickey Mouse and alerted me that they intended to question me about them at the hearing.

Question they did—more like a severe grilling.

Initially the hearing was running rather smoothly, concentrating on the lack of controls on fraud, waste, and abuse when Mrs. Spellman asked me about what she cutely had decided to call the "Walt Disney Affair." When she used that phrase, I sensed myself getting into trouble. The press immediately started the cameras rolling as if there had been a pre-arranged signal. She pointedly asked me to detail what we had done. I explained how we had punched one fictitious individual on the payroll at a salary at $99,000 per year, more than twice the $47,000 limit of the maximum federal salary. I explained that any basic system should have the control to reject such a transaction. Then I cited many of the other errors that were in our report, including non-existent charge codes, non-existent offices, erroneous social security numbers, and even the hiring of one employee whose hiring date preceded his birth date. I also carefully explained how we did not run our test "live" by using HUD's computer, but rather in the off hours with their permission. Seemingly ignoring the real issues she asked the question I knew was coming.

"And what was the exact name of the employee that we had used?"

I responded, "Donald Duck." She then asked the same questions about some of the other fictitious characters we had placed on the payroll. When I described the errors that were revealed in the document, she bored in on the names and out it came. "Mickey Mouse and Porky Pig." That did it. The press had a field day.

My guess was it must have been a slow news day. The story was not only carried on the evening TV in the Washington area, but it was on the national news as well. Even Huntley and Brinkley used it as their sign off at the end of their show, "Good night, Donald; good night, Mickey."

Unfortunately, what was lost in the hubbub and was not mentioned, was the crucial fact that our report was issued in 1975 *before* the current HUD Secretary, Patricia Harris took office. At the time, Mrs. Harris had been traveling around the country on a speech-making tour. At each of the several stops rather than being asked about her particular programs that she wanted to discuss, all the press wanted to know was how Donald Duck got on the HUD payroll. The press had also ignored my explicit testimony that it was only a test and it was run off-line in off hours, and no checks were actually issued. We had made it clear that no actual payments were made.

Of course, the press accounts made it appear as if we really had gotten Donald Duck on the payroll. Everyone jumped on the bandwagon. Johnny Carson announced on his show that he had learned there was a person in the country with the real name of Donald Duck. He was an Interior Department employee.

Secretary Harris was livid. Again, ignoring the real issues of negligence and fraud, she made numerous long distance calls back to Washington to her senior officials and just "raised hell." The press organizations were badgering my office incessantly for clarifications. I would tell each of them about off-line tests and the time frame of the study. In high journalistic fashion however, none of them were interested in *when* the report was issued, just *what* we had done and the use of the cartoon characters. Of course, Mrs. Harris was on the attack too. She even placed a direct call to Elmer Staats, the Comptroller General. She got downright nasty, I was later told. She complained that my testimony was unfair, and it was a cheap shot, maligning her and her department. This of course was even though everything in the report was true and it was issued before she took office.

The next day I got a very rare phone call. The Comptroller General called me directly to ask exactly what I was telling the press. I explained to him that I was telling them the date of the report, but they did not seem interested in that. He said he personally thought the use of the Disney characters was clever methodology, but from the tone of his voice it was clear he felt I had exaggerated the situation. I respectively disagreed.

Two days after that phone call, I was "summoned" to a meeting with Don Scantlebury, my Director, and Bill Medina, the Assistant Secretary of HUD. Medina was the big-shot so he ran the meeting. He walked us through the rebuttal testimony he planned to present at a Congressional hearing scheduled for a few days later. Scantlebury said GAO had also been asked to testify in order to "clarify the record."

Medina pulled out a big chart to purportedly downplay the failed computer section of the HUD payroll system and to emphasize the manual process the clerks went through with the documents. The chart showed many very large boxes but with the computer process, which was the guts of the system, being a very small box in the lower corner. Of course, it didn't matter to him that the multitude of errors and flaws resulted in millions being wasted. He was trying to de-emphasize the computer weaknesses.

We pointed out to him that the chart was misleading and should not be used, to which he surprisingly agreed. We also pointed out that we were aware of a draft Inspector General's report that referred to our 1975 HUD report. It took the position that our recommendations were valid but had not yet been implemented by HUD. Medina seemed embarrassed that we knew about the draft report.

Krieger, Don Scantlebury, and I met with the Comptroller General to go over the statement. We all felt we were being a bit too apologetic. It's not easy to just roll over to political pressure when you know you are in the right. Nevertheless, our statement was "adjusted" to show that the date of the report never came up nor was there ever any intention of hiding it. We inserted the statement that the tests were in fact done before the current Secretary took office. Also, that the new system being designed to correct these systemic weaknesses had not yet been fully developed. This last statement was of course untrue since even very rudimentary procedures would have prevented most of the abuses.

At the hearing we were the first witnesses and Don Scantlebury read our statement into the record. We were followed by Bill Medina, who promptly unfolded his giant chart unfairly depicting the system — the same chart which he had agreed several days before not to show. Interestingly enough, the press didn't buy his obfuscation and that evening on the national news there was a rehash of the Donald Duck story.

A few weeks later at GAO offices, I passed Henry Eschwege, the Director of the now named RECD, Resources, Economic Community and Development Division, responsible for HUD oversight. He told me that at one point the Comptroller General had chastised him for ignoring what he referred to as "bread and butter" reviews that had been brought to my Division. In other words, I was guilty of grandstanding for the Comptroller General which made him look bad.

With Eschwege now in the higher ranks of GAO management, I no longer had a highly-placed friend in court. I thought I had a good shot at upper movement to the Associate Director level, but one thing you can't do in GAO is make waves and then expect to be promoted. While I had many friends and allies who appreciated what I was doing with work on the civil agencies, I realized that I had been damaged by this event and would probably not advance within that office.

It only takes one little slip and I had slipped.

So, I would then continue to slog on to the end of my career as an Assistant Director in GAO. The hard part was watching younger junior staff members with lesser responsibilities and experience move on by into Associate Director and higher positions. But I decided to stick it out and do my best. After all, I concluded that for a kid from the other side of the tracks in New York City, I had not done too badly.

15. The First GAO Sting Operation

What two things do the companies G & A Outfitters, Gunther's Aircraft Overhaul, and Great American Outdoors have in common? First, they each have the initials GAO and secondly, they are nonexistent companies. They were created in 1982 for the first GAO Sting Operation.

Earlier that year we had begun some review work at the large, centralized payment center of the Department of Agriculture. They had set up their system in a modern, new facility in suburban New Orleans. They had some powerful connections at the Office of Management and Budget and were touting this system as the way to go for the entire Federal Government. That would have been quite a feather in the Department's cap. GAO however was concerned.

Every month the Agricultural Department processed thousands of payments for such things as equipment, office supplies, and rent. The primary objective of the new system seemed to simply make as many payments as fast as possible, thus creating the appearance of a highly efficient organization.

Our New Orleans field office team had several meetings with Clarence McShane, the Director of the new National Finance

Center. Our observations focused on internal controls. We were not alone in our apprehensions, the Department's own Inspector General already had issued several reports recommending improvement of their internal controls over payments.

One of our primary worries was a system disingenuously called the "Miscellaneous Payments System." Astoundingly, the Department considered a "miscellaneous payment" any amount up to 100,000 dollars. Their thousands of small field offices would send basic forms into the new Payment Center for processing. Receipts of documents supporting the purchase were kept at the field facilities. The National Finance Center was supposed to review the documents for accuracy and proper accounting codes as well as for an authorizing signature—not an easy task without the base paperwork. Then the payment would be made. It was clear that even this procedure was not being followed. The computer could automatically check the codes, which were easily available, but no one appeared to be checking signatures.

Guess that would be too time consuming.

There were thousands of individuals in the field that were approving officers, so we could understand why this would be a difficult task. Nonetheless, it was essential, and it was not being done.

In subsequent meetings, McShane took the attitude that the Finance Center was a new experiment, and he believed the controls were adequate. It was evident they intended to take no action. They also had completely ignored the prior recommendations by their Inspector General. It was time to try a new approach. McShane's point was that we hadn't proved any monies were lost. We were about to change that.

Upon my return to Washington after yet another unproductive visit with McShane, I met with representatives from GAO's General Counsel's office. I proposed the creation of ten fictitious companies to send bogus vouchers to the Agriculture Finance Center to see if they would be paid. New ideas for trial audits always make senior officials nervous, particularly after the "Disney Affair" and this was no exception.

However, several of our bright young lawyers liked the idea and after a series of meetings, it was approved. The only hitch was that we were not to conduct the test without notifying an official of the Department of Agriculture. This only seemed reasonable under the circumstances. We met with the Department's Assistant Secretary for Administration in his Washington office. He actually liked the idea. He had great doubts that we would succeed in our test but agreed not to alert any of his finance officials. Our New Orleans GAO staff that was doing most of the work was excited about the prospects of the test. However, to be certain we had adequate controls ourselves over the bogus payments, we decided to use our Denver office to receive the payments. After all, what we were doing was legal embezzlement.

Ten companies were created, each with the initials GAO. We even took George Orwell, author of the book *1984*, and gave him a middle initial that created the George A. Orwell Company. We obtained the blank voucher forms very easily. Hundreds of agriculture employees had access to the particular appropriation and payment codes that were to be placed on the forms. This by itself was a pretty lax procedure.

We quickly prepared 10 vouchers. I signed a number of them as did other GAO auditors. Each form required three signatures, the preparer, the auditor, and the authorizing signature. Each document also needed an address to send the payment. We used the address of GAO's Denver regional office. We were careful to put an office room number down, since no organization by that name would be listed at that address. We also included a phone number which was an unlisted number in our Denver office. We even had fun inventing nonexistent certifying officers. I took the names Clyde Beasley and Jim Masters. The payment documents were mailed to the Finance Center from several of our offices around the country in order to give them different postmarks and arrival dates. Then we held our breath and sat back and waited.

To no one's surprise, the phone at the Denver office never rang. Our staff in New Orleans was carefully watching for the payments. Upon arrival the payment documents would first be audited manually and examined. Then they were sent for computer processing and payment. Three of our transactions arrived immediately and passed the initial review without any questions. They were sent on to the computer area, but then potential disaster struck. A central malfunction in their new computer rejected an entire days transactions. The entire batch was returned to the input center, including the three bogus requests of ours. Not to worry, our three transactions were audited a second time for errors, quickly approved, and returned to the computer center system.

Within a mere eight days, all of the test payments were accepted and processed, and checks were sent to our Denver office. This was interesting since in GAO's prior work in overseeing the government's cash management, we suggest that bills be paid when due, usually thirty days. In its quest to show off its super efficiency, the Agriculture Department was not only paying bogus bills; they were paying them early.

As it turned out, during this time I had a conflict with a previously scheduled vacation. Sailing on my boat was important to me and the rest of my family. It was a way of preserving my sanity at the auditing and investigative swamp in Washington. We had a big discussion of what to do if something went wrong while I was away.

Several of my staff were also sailors and knew I had a radio/telephone on board. Our Director, Will Campbell, decided it was important that only I should be the one to decide to pull the plug if something really bad happened. I had a high morale staff that had a good sense of humor — and we occasionally liked to use it.

Dave Connor was placed in charge of reaching me. We had to set up a system of codes to describe what had happened. Placing a call to a boat through a marine radio/telephone operator is risky. All vessels or any individual with a radio receiver within 50 miles could listen in on the conversation. We arranged a system of codes to first describe the issue for me and then to advise Dave as to what to do about it.

My staff secretly hoped for a minor reason to have to call me. They had planned that after the business discussion took place, they would notify me (and all vessels within 50 miles to hear) the hoax announcement that my bank had called and since I had missed half a dozen payments on my boat, they had issued a repossession notice. Fortunately, that never happened. But if they had pulled it off, every port I pulled into for the rest of the week would recognize the boat that the bank was trying to repossess.

Dave owned up to it on my return to put a smile on my face. Luckily, they never got an opportunity to pull the ruse off. But I didn't mind too much. One thing I always believed in our line of work — If you lose your sense of humor, it's all over.

The Department of Agriculture on the other hand, did not share our sense of humor about our test. The bogus bills were paid dutifully to the Denver addresses for all 10 of the fake companies. We arranged for another meeting with Clyde McShane. The damning evidence in hand, we rehashed our concerns about the urgent need for the Department to improve control over their systems. For his part, McShane rehashed *his* position that we had still proved nothing wrong and no changes would be made. At that point, I threw the treasury checks on the table and told McShane in detail what we had done. He was furious. He wanted to know what legal right we had to conduct such a test. I referred him to his own Assistant Secretary who had authorized the test. We also informed McShane that the Senate Governmental Affairs Committee had been following our work and would be soon calling him to schedule a hearing.

We then asked McShane to rethink his plans for corrective action and headed back for Washington. One of our New Orleans based staff later informed me that McShane was seen out in the computer facility shortly after our meeting, kicking a computer. Within a few weeks it was obvious that some changes were being made. Clerks were seen busily comparing the signatures on payment documents to the signatures of certifying officers that were on file.

No word on what happened to McShane.

The next target for our investigation at the Agriculture Department was the "system" it used for paying gasoline bills. The Department had almost 25,000 vehicles, with many in rural areas—an awful lot of mileage. We were concerned because they had over 50,000 gasoline credit cards on the loose. More than *two* for every vehicle they owned. The credit cards of course would be used to purchase gas only for Government vehicles. Every month the major gasoline companies would forward a computer tape with all the charge details and bills totaling thousands of dollars to the infamous New Orleans payment center. The payment center would pay the bill without any audit or cross checks. We were concerned that there should be at least some occasional test auditing to assure abuses weren't taking place. Certainly, no government employee would use the credit cards used to pump gas into their personal cars.

We examined box after box of credit card tickets. There was a major problem. Unfortunately, most of the gasoline stations would fail to put the license number down so we could determine if it was a government vehicle. The record keeping was incredibly sloppy, but we kept pouring through charge tickets looking for abuses. We pretty much came up empty except for one very interesting charge. We thought we might have a situation of a female employee purchasing gas for personal use. Her name Lana Mower. We started searching the agriculture records to see in which office Ms. Mower was employed. By matching where the purchase was made, my staff checked with the Agriculture office in that area and inquired about the specific purchase. My staff member came back from the telephone call with a bit of a red face. He said they checked and that we had misread the charge ticket. It wasn't Ms. Lana Mower. It was "lawn mower." They had purchased a supply of gas for the lawn mowing equipment used in the upkeep of the office grounds.

Well, sometimes the GAO does not always win. This time though, even without finding fraud, the Department was convinced there was a problem with internal controls and took action and installed systems and procedures to better control the credit cards and monitor the gasoline usage of their vehicles.

16. The Energy Scandal

A quick personal note. It was the summer of 1980 and trage-dy struck GAO and my division. Don Scantlebury, our popular young Division Director, promised his wife he would go to the doctor regarding severe pain in his left arm. He never made it. The next morning on his way to work he collapsed and died. He was only 51. It was an incredible loss, and it had a profound effect on me.

There was a viewing that Friday night. Our usual Friday rou-tine was to pack up the kids and head for our 24-foot sailboat for the weekend. By coincidence, the viewing was on the way to the marina. It was very difficult to see someone in my age bracket who was my friend and boss in a casket.

Nearing the marina, there was a long line of boats, both new and used. "Lorraine, maybe we should consider getting a bigger boat?" The piercing cries of joy from the boys in the back seat was deafening.

Saturday morning, we stopped in to see a local yacht dealer I knew, and it did not take long to find a used Pearson 30 that was in pretty good shape. Given that it was end of season, the price was reasonable and he even offered us a trade—somewhat unheard of except for a new purchase. After some negotiations for additional equipment the deal was done.

It is strange how death affects some people.

It was early November 1981. At the GAO I had been on a roll as well. We had issued a number of reports on the Department of Housing and Urban Development that resulted in hundreds of millions of dollars being collected—with equal untold future amounts saved for taxpayers. Additionally, we had done several substantive audits in the departments of Agriculture, Interior, and Treasury. We had been heavily involved assisting President Carter's cash management task force where we helped make major improvements in the collection and use of the funds throughout the federal government.

Then I got another one of those calls to immediately come to GAO offices in the main building. Don Scantlebury, our Director and my friend, had been replaced by Acting Director, Will Campbell. The meeting was held with Will, Dexter Peach, a long-time personal friend who was now the Director of GAOs Energy Division, and the usual gaggle of several staff members. I was informed that there appeared to be a serious problem in the Department of Energy.

The House Government Operations Committee thought it had uncovered what amounted to be wide-spread fraud, waste, and abuse. Interestingly, they were contemplating having an oversight hearing to determine why GAO had *not* done much work investigating Energy's financial operations or management. One of the reasons we had not done much work there was GAO's growing shortage of accountants for all assignments, and the DOE's remote location about 35 miles north of Washington. Also, there was the security access problem. Many of the Department of Energy Management functions were located at the old atomic energy plant in Germantown, Maryland. Access to that facility required special, high-level clearances called "Q" or "L". Those clearances are expensive and very time consuming to procure. We were happy to take on the project but needed some form of compromise with the Committee in order to get started.

One of the things that had pushed the Committee to arrive at its conclusion to confront us was a GAO evaluator by the name of Ron. He had been assigned to assist the subcommittee staff. That had been a mistake. Ron had the reputation of being a loose cannon. Typically, he would take the slightest indication of a problem, magnify it (for his own purposes) and present it in an expanded way to his Staff Director, John Galloway, and his principal assistant, Steve Englemeyer. Galloway and Englemeyer were two of the most hell raising investigators on Capitol Hill. Many GAO officials simply did not care to deal with them. We also had been assigned another senior GAO evaluator that had a personality clash with both of them. The situation was definitely not a good one. Campbell and Peach agreed that the best approach would be to establish a joint task force from our division and theirs with me in the lead.

"Maybe we needed evaluators to evaluate the evaluators."

As of yet I had not had the pleasure of meeting Charles Bowsher, the new Comptroller General. He had only been on board a month, but I knew his background and was optimistic. He had been a partner in the accounting firm of Arthur Anderson and a former Assistant Secretary of the Navy for financial management. It would be a pleasure to have a CPA back at the helm. During the 10-year tenure of Elmer Staats, he had concentrated on expanding GAO's program evaluation capability. That focus had materially reduced the number of accountants in GAO. Accounting was centralized primarily in my division. We were terribly short-handed but under Bowsher's leadership began to expand our accounting and auditing capabilities.

Growth like that, however, doesn't happen overnight. Campbell, Peach, and I had a lengthy meeting with him to review our position on the impending evaluation of our actions. He was very supportive of the task force approach and agreed that some compromise with the Committee was necessary to avoid an oversight hearing. Tom Hagenstad, now the Office of Congressional Relations Director and I went up to meet with Galloway and Englemeyer. Galloway played the heavyweight.

As expected, he opened with a bit of a tirade about neglect of the Department of Energy by the General Accounting Office. He raised the threat of an oversight hearing critical of the GAO. He produced a laundry list of several areas that in his opinion GAO should be looking at. Many of these areas were developed by his bulldog, Ron. I had reviewed some of Ron's work before the meeting and saw a lot of things that were not properly developed or just plain wrong. I sized Galloway up as a reasonable individual but one who liked to intimidate everybody around him. I looked at the laundry list of areas and decided to take Galloway head on. I looked him square in the eye.

"John, some of this stuff is pure bullshit. It is unsupportable and it will just get you into trouble if you pursue these areas."

Galloway looked startled, but I saw a gleam in his eye and a friendly little grin at the corner of his mouth. I knew I had done the right thing. Just at that point, Hagenstad jumped in.

"I knew you'd enjoy working with Cronin, John."

Galloway continued to smile and looked at me.

"Tell me, John, do you have fun in your work?"

"Damn right I do. Do you have fun in *your* work?"

Galloway laughed and the friction melted away. I sensed we could work together toward the common good.

We agreed that the Comptroller General would testify before

their committee which was chaired by Congressman Toby Moffett. It was agreed that GAO would not be openly criticized and that we would announce the creation of a special energy task force. We further agreed to make a major commitment to review the financial management issues at the Department of Energy. I told Englemeyer and Galloway that I would develop a plan and meet with them to review it before the hearing.

Upon my return to GAO, I quickly looked over my staff roster. As the Director of this task force, I would need two strong lieutenants. I selected Jim Kracheyk and Chris Martin. Kracheyk had worked closely with me on several projects and had become my right-hand man. Martin was very skilled in the use of computers and analyzing computer systems. I met with Dexter Peach and he supplied a man named Tom Hack and several other senior people. I built up a Washington team totaling about 15 people. We developed a plan to use the support of five of our regional offices as well.

We began by looking in general at accounting and financial management, property management, and in particular, the operations of the Strategic Petroleum Reserve. We got in touch with the DOE Assistant Secretary, Bill Hefflefinger, who promised full cooperation. I arranged a meeting with Hefflefinger and explained I needed some expedited clearances for the personnel that would be assigned. Moffett's Committee wanted the entire project completed in six to nine months. That was no easy task for GAO, particularly to undertake such a major comprehensive review of an entire Department.

The hearing went smoothly, and we came out with our marching orders. I enjoyed the opportunity to testify with new Comptroller General Bowsher. On board only a short period of time, nevertheless he had an excellent awareness of the organization. He had done his homework. He knew I was the GAO liaison to the White House and was aware of a lot of the work I had done. In preparation for the hearing, I had the opportunity to discuss with him many of those projects. I sensed that he was a little concerned about the hearing since it was his second one as Comptroller General. Fortunately, the hearing came off well and he was very pleased. That opened up a direct line of communication between the two of us that would last for years.

Because of the lead time required, the first thing on my agenda was the issuance of the security clearances. I arranged a meeting with GAO's Security Office. They were not much help. Based on their prior experiences, they made getting the Energy clearances seem like a hopeless if not impossible task. They gave me some time frames that made it appear it would take months just to get people cleared so they could start work. That obviously was unacceptable. We would never have been able to come close to meeting our mandated time frame. I called DOE Assistant Secretary Hefflefinger who put me in touch with their head of security and a meeting was arranged. The Director of Security at Energy was very helpful and pointed out to me that, in fact, their security office was not the problem. GAO's security office was the problem. They seemed to always have tremendous difficulty getting the initiating paperwork from GAO's security office.

I returned to GAO and personally supervised the new staff members from both divisions in filling out the required clearance forms. I alerted the teams that there could be some difficulties with our own security office, so they were prepared. I visited our Security Office with a large box containing all the required forms. Sure enough, I immediately ran into a bureaucratic review process. They sat me down and told me how things would work. I replied that as I had made other arrangements, everything was all set. They merely had to certify that these were

GAO employees that had been previously cleared and provide a certification of the clearances they held. I had already taken care of the rest. Quite an argument followed during which I was told I had no business even going to Energy's Security Office. I gave them the box of completed paperwork and told them to do it now the way I asked, or I would go directly to the Comptroller General.

Within hours of that meeting, one of our security officers visited our division head to complain that I was being somewhat obnoxious. Will Campbell was waiting—and prepared. The individual was informed we were sorry for their hurt feelings but in fact they were the problem and that they had better move the paperwork as quickly as possible just the way I had told them.

"One small victory over a bureaucrat."

The security officer later called me to try to explain why she had been told to make a visit to the division. I told her I knew why she made the visit to the division—and it did not work.

"Just sign the damn paperwork and let me get it up to the department so I can get on with my job."

Reluctantly they did, and the clearances amazingly breezed through. In fact, all of our people were given immediate temporary access to the facility until the permanent security badges were arranged. That was something our Security Office said would never happen. I knew differently from my stints having worked at the Treasury's Bureau of Engraving and Printing and at the White House. Those experiences of working in cleared areas came in very handy to break through the bureaucracy.

Martin, Kracheyk, and I burned the midnight oil for a couple of weeks to come up with an overall plan for the work in the five regional offices that we had selected. We knew that with all the various Energy facilities around the country, we would not be spending very much time at home, so we made plans for extensive travel. Lorraine was not particularly pleased.

We completed the entire review in less than eight months and that included two full hearings before Congressman Moffett's Subcommittee. Our investigations revealed that the principal concerns that the Subcommittee had about the lack of financial management were totally justified—and was widespread in all three major areas of the Department of Energy (DOE). The Department's operational accounting was horrendous. Its accounting controls for property were non-existent and the management of the nation's Strategic Petroleum Reserve was a disaster.

Interestingly, we found that the DOE did have a lot of activities that produced pretty nice income. In fact, they collected about 78,000 dollars a day in receipts. However, the control over that income was nonexistent. They were not even sure it had accounted for all of its money. Their computerized systems were in chaos. One simple element of control over a computerized system of course, is access through passwords. Most of DOE passcodes had been compromised with the exception of only the most secure weapons systems. Cash expenditures to oil license/lease grantees were out of control. The Department had provided 23 million dollars in *excess* cash to its grantees during a one-year period. In most cases the government's cash was to be invested to earn interest for the grantee. But often when the field work was finished, Energy would not perform what was called a Closeout and recover the monies not spent on the project. Millions in taxpayer money was lost.

To make matters worse, we found very poor regulation over the hundreds of millions of dollars of Departmental-owned property. We discovered a difference between records and inventories that showed an unaccounted-for loss of about 187 million dollars in property. In one example, expensive drill pipe was being purchased regularly for use at the Strategic Petroleum Reserve (SPR) while at the same time substantial amounts of unused and excess used drill pipe lay stored in the Arizona desert. Management and procurement at the SPR were particularly out of control. We suspected but were unable to prove any widespread fraud.

Fraud or just negligence?

Reviewing the SPR was certainly an interesting and complex project. Luckily, I had the team to do it. The main purpose of the reserves was to provide a supply of oil for the nation in case of national emergency. Nature had created large caverns of salt deposits under the Louisiana coast. Secure storage areas were created in these huge salt domes. They were made by pumping in hot water that would then leach out the salt and create a huge cavern into which the nation's oil reserves would be pumped.

The SPR frequently had many visiting national and international dignitaries, fascinated to see this technological marvel. To impress them, the SPR had created a room-sized illuminated display showing in glowing detail how the oil was flowing and current capacities. When we checked into it, the whole display was a phony front and none of the sensing and measuring devices had been hooked up. They were merely programmed to look as if something was happening.

Another example of poor management and planning had created an added unbelievable situation. The expensive valves that were installed at the top of each dome to pump the oil in were only one-way valves. Incredibly, no provision had been made to pump the oil out. The DOE had to spend hundreds of thousands of dollars to have the valves replaced with valves that were capable of pumping the oil out.

Brilliant!

We also determined that another very costly part at the SPR were the drill bits used to drill into the salt domes. In one case, employees were removing the worn, unusable drill bits. The bits then were refurbished by an outside firm. These rehabbed drill bits were then sold back to the SPR as *new* drill bits. We turned that one over to the Department's Inspector General and to the Justice Department as well. I don't recall anybody being prosecuted or ever going to prison. Just another example of the frustrating side of uncovering white collar crime in government activities throughout the years. I guess there is just a general attitude that it is ok to steal from the government.

At the conclusion of the field work, Jim Kracheyk, Chris Martin, and myself met with Jim Reed of the DOE who was assigned as our liaison. We made a tour through all of the energy offices, laid out our findings, and discussed possible recommendations and remedies. It didn't take long before Reed was on our side. We did have some strange meetings in which we encountered the usual resistance to our findings. When we presented a summary of our results at the San Francisco DOE office, at the conclusion of my briefing, the official in charge made the comment, "Well, I guess the union is safe." I was not sure if he was referring to the workers or the nation. But to me, the sarcasm showed a complete lack of interest in improving the financial management of the Department or the Federal Government for that matter.

Then we visited DOE's Chicago Office of Finance to specifically discuss all the amounts due to Energy, and the receivables that had never been recorded on the books. One of their officials commented, "Why record an account receivable on the books, after all we collect them." At that moment, Reed just put his head in his hands.

We continued our whirlwind visits to the various SPR offices around the country. Late each night I phoned Lorraine to tell her the end was nearly in sight—at least I hoped so. I had been through 11 airports in nine days and was getting a little frazzled around the edges. The reason was simple, as shown by this example.

At the beginning of one of the final meetings at a large SPR office the following exchange took place. The executive in charge of procurement bragged that this was the best procurement system ever developed by any federal agency. It was even better than the outstanding system he had worked on before he came to Energy. I was more than somewhat irritated by this. That did not get the meeting off to a good start.

"What procurement system did you work on before?"

"Why do you ask that?"

"Simple. This place is so screwed up I want to find out where you worked previously. It has got to be even worse than this and I want to get my team of investigators over there as soon as possible."

On our return to Washington, we briefed Galloway and Englemeyer. They generally were pleased with what we had found, however John Galloway in particular wished to pursue the SPR problems even harder—especially in the areas of fraud and abuse. They decided to make their own field visits and spent a week interviewing at various SPR offices. In the middle of the week, they asked me to fly out and join them at the SPR headquarters in New Orleans.

Ernie Candalora was the GAO Audit Manager in charge of our work in that city for the project. Upon my arrival, Ernie and I spent a very unpleasant day with Galloway and Englemeyer. In essence they wanted us to become detectives, spending time at the location trying to ferret out each and every individual case of fraud and abuse. We refused. We spent half the day shouting at each other. At one point, they threatened to call the Comptroller General. That was the final straw. I told Galloway I had his direct number and would be happy to get him on the phone. Galloway could see that I was angry. Fortunately, he backed down, realizing that he was not going to win.

Ernie and I had known each other for many years, and we made a good team. Prior to the trip, Ernie had indicated he had a friend with a brand-new sailboat who would like me to go out with them to give them the benefit of some of my experience. We had planned an evening sail after work on Lake Poncetrain. I suspected it would be a long day with Galloway and Englemeyer so I threw some old sailing clothes in the trunk of the rental car as I left the hotel early that morning. I was right. It was a miserable day with Galloway and Englemeyer.

Sometimes these jobs however do have their lighter side. After all the arguing was finished, I headed for the marina at Lake Poncetrain. Ernie stopped at his house to change and then was to join me there. I drove to the marina and parked the rental car on an unused side of the parking lot. I slipped into the back seat and began to change. There had been some vehicles and cars over on the other side of the parking lot. As I was changing, suddenly there was a tremendous crash which dramatically shook the car and knocked me to the floor. I had just been hit by a truck backing up from across the way, attempting to turn around and exit the parking lot. Of course, I was only in my undershorts at the time. The driver jumped out of his cab and was very apologetic. I climbed out of my wrecked car hopping around as I struggled to pull up and adjust my sailing pants. Naturally the driver did not want the incident on his insurance policy, so he drove to the rental place to tell them what had happened, and they took care of the arrangements. Ernie arrived a moment or two later and seeing the taillights and bumper laying all over the parking lot just broke into total laughter. It had been that kind of a day.

Finally, we got things worked out with Galloway and Englemeyer and finalized our preparations for the hearings before Congressman Moffett. Surprisingly, the hearings went smoothly. The Department of Energy testified and agreed to take corrective actions on each and every one of the matters we had uncovered. The Comptroller General was very pleased with the hearings and said a lot of complementary things as we drove back to the General Accounting Office in his car. With one minor exception.

Comptroller Bowsher was very conservative. There was a humorous exchange at the hearings that he was a little uncomfortable with. One of the more irreverent Congressman on the Committee was Barney Frank. Frank looked and sounded a lot like the comedian Buddy Hackett. As we were describing the problem with the pipe in the desert being unused, Frank interrupted me. He pointed out that earlier in the morning they had a lengthy hearing on the nation's surplus cheese and that they could find no place to store the cheese.

"Maybe the government could store the cheese in the pipes in the desert."

Having visited the site and taken many pictures, I had seen a large jack rabbit population—I fired back.

"I'm not certain of that, Congressman, you see they have a jack rabbit problem in the desert and I would be concerned that the rabbits would eat the cheese."

Frank and the rest of the Committee chuckled. I sensed that the Comptroller General was a little irritated at my lack of decorum. I probably should have kept my mouth shut, but it is hard for an Irishman to resist a golden opportunity for a little Irish wit.

17. The Investigation Of The CPA Profession

I had been pretty happy during the 12 years I ran the Civil Agency Audit Group. We were located across town from the main GAO building, which was fine given my independent streak. In fact, I had spent most of my 28 years in GAO working outside of the main building. The building had been erected in 1951 with a totally different type of function in mind. It was designed as a carryover from all the voucher audits from World War II. The building had been cut up into so many little offices the air flow system did not work well—nor did the air conditioning! Not working at headquarters was a blessing as they would find too many staff and other non-project related functions for me to do. Preparing other peoples' speeches, writing articles, and other administrative BS which I intensely disliked. I wanted to be on the line and enjoyed it. I didn't realize it fully at the time, but 12 years was too long to be in any one position. I was getting a little bored and probably slowing down a bit.

Sometime around mid-August of 1984, I got a phone call to come to the main building see our new Director, Fred Wolf. Fred was a very dynamic individual. He had been brought in from the same accounting firm that the Comptroller General came from, Arthur Andersen, where he was known as "The Maverick Partner."

... and that suited me just fine.

I was asked to come to Fred's office as soon as possible. No reason was given for the meeting. Those kinds of request were not usually good news. It frequently indicated one of two things; I was going to be given a job I didn't like or get my ass chewed for something I did. I guess over the years my skin got a little tougher and I did not worry as much about summons to the GAO building. After all, at this point in my career, I was well established and only about five years from retirement.

On my way to Fred's office, I bumped into our Director of Congressional Relations, a close personal and sailing friend, Tom Hagenstad. Tom took me aside and related that Fred was going to tell me about a decision the Comptroller General has made. He is going to ask you to do a review of the CPA profession. The review was personally requested by Congressman Brooks.

"Take it John, it will be a great job for your career and your future."

Although not entirely sure those few words necessarily were true, I headed for the meeting. As I mentioned, Fred and I were cut a bit from the same irreverent cloth. He would periodically kid me about my "network" of insiders. When I entered his office, he gave me a little smile and he shut the door and set me down on the couch.

"Alright, Cronin, you pride yourself on knowing what the hell is going on around here, tell me if you can what I'm going to talk to you about."

I looked at Fred and he had that little grin on his face that said I got ya this time.

"Fred, this wouldn't have something to do with the Brooks request on CPA audit quality, would it?" The smile was gone from his face.

"How the hell did you find out about this? Even your boss doesn't know about it. The final decision was just made at about 8 o'clock last night!"

I just smiled and said, "Fred, that just shows the value of a good network."

Then Fred laid it on me. So much for the pleasantries. The Chairman of the House Government Operations Committee had asked GAO to undertake a nationwide review of the quality of governmental audits as performed by local certified public accountants. These outsourced audits were of those governmental units in receipt of federal funds. There were thousands of them. Most federal laws required grant recipients to receive audits by CPAs to assure they were spending the money for their intended purpose. Because of the magnitude, the federal Inspectors General and the various agency program people relied on these outside auditors for oversight purposes. In recent years, numerous complaints had been filed that the audits were of extremely poor quality.

Fred's request was not good news. I was very anxious. Most of the senior staff in our Division were now CPAs and members of the profession. I thought it was one of the great high points in my life when I successfully completed the CPA examination. I was proud of that title. Now I was in charge of going after my fellow professionals for alleged substandard work. Some of the work was even done by the firm that the Comptroller General and Fred Wolf had come from. Despite Lorraine's perfectly mixed martinis, I spent a restless night and decided to drop by for a follow-up with Fred the next morning.

Basically, I said to Fred, "Why me?" Fred was never one to pay a lot of compliments. He just looked at me and said, "It's simple, John, the Comptroller General and I feel that you're the best individual in the organization to do the job. The only one with enough guts to do it fairly and objectively and not be influenced by the profession." There is not much one can say to a comment like that. So, I headed back to my office to begin the work of the new Audit Quality Task Force (AQTF). It was clear my tour with the Systems Audit Group was now over. I had started the unit from scratch and built it up into a thriving audit organization. It was a sad moment.

By coincidence, several months before I had been sent to an executive development school. My deputy, Jim Kracheyk had inquired about the school, since he was also going to have to attend. I told him about one of the exercises that was very interesting. I called it the "in-basket" exercise. The theory was you arrive on a new job on a Saturday when no one is around. The manager's in-basket has been left for you to go through and sort out and prioritize. The assignment is to make management decisions including personnel, staffing, and other problem cases.

During additional discussions with Fred, I asked what would happen to my old group. It was important to me that it continue under excellent leadership. He asked for my suggestion as to who should take it over. Instantly I suggested Jim. He agreed and told me that was his choice also.

Fred wanted me to get moving and relocate to the GAO building immediately because several months had gone by since Congressman Brooks had made the official request. To complicate matters, it had been the subject of much discussion within the Comptroller General's office and even in the halls of Congress. When I got back, I picked up my in-basket and walked into Jim's office. I always remember the look on his face when he asked what the meeting at GAO was about. I told him and asked him if he remembered my discussion about the famous in-desk exercise. He said he did, and I handed him my in-basket and said, "Well, it's for real. Now things are in your capable hands. Good luck, Jim," and I headed for GAO and the new audit assignment.

My first order of business was to immediately begin a search for new staff members for my AQTF. It was a delicate task for a delicate project. I came up with three very strong individuals for the core of the team, Leslie Aronovitz, Marv Doyal, and Dave Clark. I had started out with only Marv and Leslie. But not too long afterwards, Marv had the opportunity to leave for another position and Dave joined as one of my two principal deputies.

I began my work reviewing the history of how the CPA profession handled criticism—not well it turned out. They were a powerful organization with powerful lobbyists. The question of substandard auditing had of course been raised by Congress before. It also had been raised by GAO before and even previously had been raised by the Inspector Generals. Each time, the very powerful profession took the position that the substandard audits that were identified were extremely isolated cases and did not reflect on the profession as a whole. But this time they had no idea with whom they were dealing. That said, even I knew I had my work cut out for me.

Wanting to hit the ground running, I began reviewing a previous study I found that had been prompted by complaints from numerous Inspector Generals. They had forwarded over 100 cases of substandard audits to the ethics division of the American Institute of Certified Public Accountants (AICPA) for review. I found their interim report but no final report. By chance it was now just a few weeks from the huge annual meeting of the AICPA. The meeting was scheduled at the Hyatt Regency hotel in Atlanta. It was a meeting that GAO encouraged it's senior CPAs to attend, so I was no stranger to the event. As a courtesy, Fred Wolf had called the president of the AICPA to tip him off about our work.

Not sure that was a good idea.

I relayed a request to the association president asking for a meeting to discuss a series of documents including the missing final report of the ethics division. Fred, along with Jack Adair, the Associate Director to whom I was reporting, and I met with the leadership of the AICPA. I asked about the number of substandard governmental audits the ethics division had examined in the last three years. They seemed very cordial. They were not happy with the investigation but promised their assistance. Amazingly, when I asked for the final report of the ethics division on the IG's cases, they presented it to me.

One major problem — the report was dated the day before our meeting. It was clear the whole thing was a ruse. The study had died at the AICPA for lack of interest only to be rushed together for a final report as a result of my request. We were furious. When I asked them about the number of substandard audits they had reviewed in the last three years, their response was 11. What a crock! I couldn't believe it — that out of a universe of about 20,000 audits per year there were only 11 bad ones in three years. No wonder they were so cordial.

Fortunately, my work on putting together the energy task force several years earlier helped immensely in forming this group. Leslie, Dave, and I formulated a plan. We knew the Inspector Generals were doing some work in the area, however there was no central record keeping. We devised a way to identify the CPA audits they had reviewed at 46 of their locations. First, we knew they had looked into about 10,000 audits and we could obtain those findings. Second, we would select our own sample of 150 audits that had not been reviewed by the IG's. We would visit the CPA firms' offices and review their working papers to see if their audits were up to par. We had agreed that any substandard audits we identified would be referred to the State Boards of Accountancy or the Ethics Division of the AICPA for disciplinary action.

That would have been a great procedure but for the fact that the discipline (or the lack of it) by the State Boards of Accountancy and the AICPA themselves was a serious problem. Normally, we would receive no feedback, or if we did, we found out very little if any action was taken. In fact, one case I referred in 1979 was not resolved for nearly ten years.

The high sensitivity of this project became clear early on—and it was growing. I would be dealing with Congressman Brooks' key staffers, Rick Barnes and Chris Cooper. They were very queasy about GAO even undertaking this review. It was evident they felt that we were going to be biased on the side of the profession. They were generally pleased with my appointment as I had known them and worked with them on the White House reviews for a number of years. By the time we staffed up in Washington and six of our regional offices, we had almost 120 GAO auditors assigned to the task force. I insisted that the key people in each of our regional offices be CPAs. At that time, many of our people were not CPAs because of a change in emphasis on professional disciplines in GAO during the Staats administration.

Obviously, it would be difficult for non-CPAs to properly recognize issues and file charges against practicing CPAs. Unfortunately, it was also easy to sense the "professional courtesy" issue, making many of our people nervous about reviewing the work of CPAs and criticizing them.

To combat this possible bias, we developed a program and a methodology for reviewing the CPA work papers. I organized a three-day conference in Denver to teach the assigned staff how to look for the red flags in reviewing CPA's working papers. The meeting was a good ice breaker, leading the team to a much greater confidence level. I was pleased Fred Wolf, our new Division Director, spent most of the time with us, expressing his confidence in us. This was the first time any of the staff had the opportunity to meet and deal with Fred.

After two days of technical presentations, on the third day I had lined up some guest speakers. The best was Chuck Dempsey, the former Inspector General of the Department of Housing and Urban Development. He gave everyone a good charge telling them about all the substandard CPA work he had uncovered and how some of the people he had assigned to the work were also not CPAs.

Another of the more memorable speakers was a young, attractive CPA by the name of Sally Thompson. I invited Sally because she was an active member of the National Association of State Boards of Accountancy and she also served on the Colorado State Board of Accountancy. Sally explained how the state boards function and their high interest in our review. She left about eighty GAO auditors in the conference room with their mouths open when she concluded her presentation.

"If you identify any substandard CPAs practicing in the state of Colorado, you turn them over to me and I will take their certificate away."

Her statements hit home, particularly for the CPAs in the audience. If there was ever any doubt as to how serious and sensitive this review was, Sally Thompson certainly made it clear.

Our first phase was the Inspectors General reports, and the results quickly came rolling in. My task force reviewed a representative sample of 10,000 of their reports and found out that about 20 percent of them were substandard. We prepared a report to Congressman Brooks and even testified at a hearing as to the causes of the substandard audits. In most cases, the CPAs simply did not know what they were doing or worse, had inexperienced personnel using governmental audits as summer fill in or training work. Unlike a tax client or an SEC registrant where a CPA can get in trouble with the IRS or the SEC, there was little risk in a routine governmental audit. This often enticed questionable CPAs and procedures into the arena.

Next came our reviews of the CPAs. We selected 150 cases in our six regions. Soon after we started, we came across a number of substandard audits. The primary factor a CPA uses to justify his or her work is to prepare detailed working papers showing the evidence of the tests the CPA performed.

Examples would be confirmation of bank balances, analysis of liabilities and legal actions. When a review was complete, the audit would be classified as A: all ok, B: some minor problems, C: corrective action needed or D: severely substandard needing referral to the State Board of Accountancy for disciplinary action.

We were surprised that in some cases, there were no work papers at all or very few. They had merely issued their opinion on the financial statements and expressed views on the adequacy of compliance with the terms and conditions of the federal grant agreement—and had done so with little or no work. The bottom line was that an astounding 34% of the governmental audits in the country were substandard.

The number even shocked the AICPA. One of their Senior Vice Presidents, Tom Kelly, in looking at the report which I shared with him just before it was released, acknowledged to me they would have to do something about it. Much to my surprise, they did. They also knew they had to respond to Congressman Brooks.

Even before the issuance of our reports, the AICPA had established a high-powered task force to review the quality of governmental audits. An associate of mine in the profession, Hal Steinberg, a partner with the firm of Peat Marwick, was appointed the task force chairman. Over the years, I developed a lot of respect for Hal and his dedication to try to help straighten out the problems besetting our profession.

Despite enduring two congressional hearings and issuing two reports to the public, plus a lot more work in progress, I was "volunteered" for the speech-making circuit. Many of the professional organizations and the state CPA societies as well as the boards of accountancy were anxious to hear what I had to say. Speaking to large groups like that is wonderful for the ego but horrible for the waistline. Between the simultaneous audit quality work and the Iran/Contra Committee investigations, I had managed to gain 25 pounds. Lorraine saw to it that I would ultimately lose the weight—with a lot of exercise and a diet involving fewer martinis.

The most troublesome and sensitive of the work was how to take action on the 57 CPAs we had identified as doing substandard work. We sent their names with letters of complaint to the 15 state boards of accountancy in whose jurisdiction the CPAs were located. My name and telephone number was placed on the referrals for the CPAs and state boards to contact if there were questions. In retrospect, that was probably a mistake and was certainly not very pleasant. Unfortunately, when the IGs did their work on reviewing CPA audits, they were not taken seriously. The most severe thing that would happen would be the CPA would get a letter from a regional Inspector General telling him or her what they had found, and would they please do it correctly the next time.

Initially when we did our reports, we were treated much the same as the IGs. We were not taken very seriously. However, when

Memoirs of the Gatekeeper

copies of our referral letters arrived at the offending CPAs, suddenly all hell broke loose. I received several interesting and some nasty phone calls. Luckily, I was pretty thick skinned after almost 30 years of auditing and investigating. In some of these calls even my ancestry was questioned, my parentage was questioned, and some pretty strong language was used about the referrals process itself. Interestingly, almost all of the CPAs that called me to complain suffered from one common illness—amnesia.

In each case our people would review the Standards of Violations. That is our professional standards bible and the basis for field work and reporting that a CPA is required to follow. Each transgressing CPA had the same argument.

"But your staff told me I did a wonderful job on the audit. They never said I did anything wrong. Why do I have this letter now after you have complained about me?"

My audit teams were well prepared. They were required simply to follow the standard procedures. On each review they prepared a detailed write-up of the exit conference with management. In each case I referred the CPA to the date of the meeting and read the memorandum of what our people said and the CPA's exact response. I would usually get an answer like, "Oh, yes I vaguely remember that meeting now." That would usually end their complaint and clear the way for any possible sanctions or penalties.

I was not thrilled particularly about going after my associates in the profession, but I guess somebody had to clean things up. The rank and file CPAs in the profession gave our reports a lot of attention. There were numerous articles in the professional journals warning the CPAs about the problems we found.

One of the more amusing dialogues was with Joe Moraglio, one of the AICPA's Vice Presidents. We had identified a lot of violations of what is called the "due professional care" standard. We talked about errors in financial statements and general sloppiness in the preparation of work. Moraglio was particularly interested in this area. He said that he was preparing an article for the Journal of Accountancy, the AICPA professional magazine. If we could furnish them with all the types of errors we saw the CPAs committing, they could publish them. In this way the CPAs could see the errors being committed on the government audits and try to avoid them in the future.

Seemed like a good idea to me…

I started discussing some of the particulars with Moraglio. I doubted he was really ready for it, but I began with some of the more grievous errors.

"Joe, for example, the opening balance of one year should agree with the closing balance of the prior year—too often, they don't."

"Hmmm—I understand."

"And that interfund transfers to and from other funds should zero out and they don't.

"I understand."

Then I said, "Joe, the left side of the balance sheet does not equal the right side of the balance sheet."

At that point Joe lost it. He screamed, "I can't print that in the Journal of Accountancy! If they're that bad, they are too far gone for us to help."

Needless to say, the article never appeared in the Journal of Accountancy.

Another very memorable meeting on a substandard audit actually involved Hal Steinberg's firm. He had phoned and said that the senior partner of their New York office, Jack Miller, wanted a meeting to review their C rating. Hal and Jack personally went over the work papers with me. They were not happy with what they saw and promised to take the necessary corrective action.

"Not so fast, gentlemen." I handed them two more sets of B rated workpapers. Though demoralized, they agreed to make the additional changes.

Several weeks later, I received a copy of the new Peat, Marwick Internal Practices Bulletin which had been distributed throughout the firm. In very concrete language it contained detailed instructions on how to follow our recommendations.

Score one for the Gipper.

My work in overseeing the CPA profession would be my last hurrah in the General Accounting Office. I guess I came into the profession virtually unknown but had remedied that situation in spades. When I left I was certainly known by most.

18. "Marcosgate"—The Investigation Of Ferdinand And Imelda Marcos

It has been estimated that during the 25-year rule of the Philippine Republic by Ferdinand and Imelda Marcos, they stole about eight billion dollars from the Philippine people. To paraphrase the words of Winston Churchill, "Never have so few stolen so much from so many." That was the statement I gave to the press at the close of the Marcos investigation and hearings.

Congressman Solarz, chairman of the Asian Pacific Affairs Committee of the House Foreign Affairs Committee, played a major role in toppling the corrupt Marcos government. I worked for months with this dedicated hard-working Congressman and his staff to pursue his beliefs while setting aside considerable abuse he took from other Congressional members.

It was early January 1986. My staff and I had not taken much time off during the Christmas holidays. We were busy drafting the second report to Congress on the status of the CPA profession's improvements on government accounting matters. Our field offices had completed their work and had forwarded the papers to us.

The most difficult part of the job, keeping the field offices on track, was over. It was no easy task to prepare such a sensitive report showing the GAO was not in bed with the profession. At least the frequent trips back and forth to the regional offices were over and we could concentrate on preparing the report.

As usual, these chapters begin with a call from my Director, in this case, Fred Wolf. On entering Fred's office, it was another one of those meetings where he shut the door. Usually not a good sign. I knew something important was brewing.

"John," he asked me, "what do you know about this Congressional investigation of Ferdinand and Imelda Marcos?"

I told him I recalled reading in the newspaper that there were allegations that the Marcos' had invested money taken from the Philippine government into personally owned properties in New York City. Fred told me that the House Foreign Affairs Committee had requested assistance from GAO in the Marcos investigation. They wanted a senior person who could analyze the accounting records and if necessary present testimony to their committee. It was that last part that made me nervous. When anyone mentions the GAO testifying before a Congressional committee, the field of candidates suddenly gets very limited — to like, guess who?

Fred knew my work and the way I had handled myself in past instances before other Congressional committees. He, being new to GAO, had no institutional biases and did not hold the Donald Duck episode against me as others in the organization had. We agreed that my deputy director on the task force, Dave Clark, would finish processing the report on the CPA profession and I would begin splitting my time between GAO and the Foreign Affairs Committee.

Normally when the GAO is assigned to work with a Congressional committee, it liaisons with one of the senior staffers or in some cases the subcommittee staff director. In this instance, however, I was told to report directly to Congressman Solarz' office. Over at the Longworth House Office Building I met with him and the committee staff director, Stanley Roth. Also present was the Congressman's administrative assistant, Michael Lewen. I was welcomed on board and given a small desk right in chairman Solarz's suite of offices. As an indication of the importance of the inquiry, he had other staff members and several additional secretaries working on a part-time basis.

Interestingly, this investigation had started with an article in a New York newspaper, The Village Voice. I never gave much credibility to that paper and I was surprised to see the level of detail in the article. There were purportedly at least five New York City office buildings owned by Ferdinand and Imelda Marcos. The investigators on the report had done an amazing amount of leg work scouring thousands of records of various agencies of the New York City government.

I have to admit I could certainly empathize with this level of tedium.

The committee thus far had focused its investigation on two brothers, Joseph and Ralph Bernstein of New York City. Joseph was a lawyer and Ralph was not, but they both were employees in the law firm of Bernstein, Carter, and Dayo. They also held positions in a real estate management company called the New York Land Company.

The Committee already had subpoenaed boxes of documents from several banks and various Bernstein companies relative to the New York properties. I was assigned the task to review the accounting aspects of the documents and to identify any further indications of ownership by the Marcos. Also, I was to identify the chain of ownership for each of the properties. This alone was daunting given the number of dummy entities both offshore and domestic. Finally, I needed to review the transcripts of the initial hearings that had been held in early December.

At those proceedings the Bernsteins had basically refused to testify, claiming attorney/client relationships. As a result of their refusal to testify, the House Committee had voted a contempt citation against them. Although I'm not a lawyer it was pretty clear the evidence as developed at the hearings was largely circumstantial. To complicate matters two Republican members of the Committee turned to vicious attacks on Chairman Solarz. Congressmen Solomon and Roth constantly badgered him about trying to adversely affect the government of the Philippines using "unsupported circumstantial evidence," and referred to his investigation as a "witch hunt." Fortunately, the ranking minority member of the committee, Jim Leach, sided with the Chairman on the need for the investigation to proceed.

With that as backdrop, I dove into the records that had accumulated so far. I started with the Lindenmere estate. Built in the early 1900's it was a huge, thirteen acre gated property right on the Northern shore of Long Island Sound. The estate had been purchased for about $400,000 and had been refurbished for over two million dollars. Most of the funding for the procurement and rehabilitation came through offshore corporations in the Netherlands Antilles and several in Panama.

Using offshore corporations was an excellent way of hiding true ownership and sources of funding. Once we traced monies back to the corporate account we hit a brick wall since those countries generally would not cooperate in providing information on the ultimate beneficial owners. But in reviewing the records compiled to date on Lindenmere, something was bothering me. It was clear something was missing from the records. Then it hit me. The taxes!

Who was paying the taxes on the property? Tax records are usually public records and easily obtained. I immediately called a Teresa Young in the Treasury's office in Suffolk County, New York. A tax search was completed and forwarded to me.

I got quite a surprise.

A number of the taxes had been paid by Anchor Holding Company, which just happened to be one of the offshore companies created by the Bernsteins. However, seven of the tax bills had been paid by a certain Vilma Bautista—and that name rang a bell. I had seen it in the records I had reviewed. I went back through the documents, and there it was. Ms. Bautista was an employee at the Philippine mission of the United Nations. She listed her address as 15 East 66th Street in New York City and that was the townhouse owned by the Philippine government. It was the primary place the Marcos' stayed when they visited New York. I contacted the State Department and was informed that Vilma Bautista was the First Secretary at the Philippine Mission to the United Nations, and as such was accorded full diplomatic immunity. My investigation also uncovered that she acted as Mrs. Marcos' personal secretary whenever she visited the United States.

We also obtained, through subpoenas, four letters from the architect and contractors who did the rehabilitation work on the estate. The architect was having trouble getting his invoices paid from the Anchor Holding Company. He had written several letters to Mrs. Marcos, all of which were delivered to the 66th Street residence. Some of them were personally delivered to Ms. Bautista.

Just as things were beginning to look promising, I was now about to run into my first roadblock in the way of—or lack of—cooperation from other government agencies. I knew that most U.S. companies doing business with foreign investors are required to file an annual report with the Department of Commerce.

Within that report, they are given a choice. They can either identify the ultimate beneficial owners of the investments or identify their country of origin. In one folder of subpoenaed records from one of the corporations, I noticed a copy of this report that identified the ultimate beneficial owners as being Philippine citizens. I contacted the Bureau of the Census in the Commerce Department and was referred to the particular assistant secretary's office that was responsible for the Census Bureau. What then followed was a number of conference calls back and forth with the Assistant Secretary, census officials, and officials of the General Counsel's office of the Department.

Having worked frequently over the years with Census data, I was well aware that by federal law, census information is confidential. An individual report cannot be released even for the most sensitive of law enforcement investigations. That said, some Census data can be obtained if it is in aggregated form. I explained repeatedly to the Department that I was not interested in obtaining information from the individual reports. I merely wanted to know if the seven operations we had specifically identified to date had filled out the required reports. The Census Bureau, however, took the position that even telling me who filed and who did not violated the statute. The statute also provided a ten thousand dollar fine and a one-year prison sentence for companies intentionally failing to file the report. It was clear I was getting a bureaucratic run around.

Time to bring in some Congressional muscle.

I got the feeling the Bureau thought they were dealing with a young inexperienced Congressional staffer, particularly since my voice sounds rather youthful over the phone. I let them know otherwise. I told them I was prepared to have a subpoena issued demanding the Secretary of Commerce appear before our subcommittee to explain why the department was protecting non-filers who would be subject to criminal prosecution. Unmoved, they said they wanted a formal request. By this time, I was furious. I told them to send someone to the Congressman's office in an hour and they would have their request. I dictated a stern letter reiterating my request and reminding the Department we would consider a subpoena for the Secretary of Commerce to appear. The letter was typed and signed by Chairman Solarz—I was pretty pleased with myself.

An hour later, the Commerce Department's legislative liaison arrived. He was more than a little surprised at my age and experience. I was still livid over the lack of cooperation and the bureaucratic atmosphere I was finding at the Department. I handed the letter to the legislative liaison and whispered a message in his ear. "Tell your boss we are not fooling around. We are very damned serious about this subpoena."

Within two hours I had a call from Commerce's General Counsel and the Assistant Secretary. It seemed the atmosphere had changed. They were now very apologetic. Unfortunately, although the Secretary was out of the country, they also would like to do everything possible to avoid his testifying at the hearing. They indicated they would try to figure out a method of giving me what I wanted without me violating any census statutes. I didn't think that should be too hard. It was Friday, and the next hearing was scheduled for the following Tuesday. That afternoon I was called in by Congressman Solarz who asked for an update. I told him about the Commerce records, the tax records, and the direct tie into Vilma Bautista. Then he dropped a bombshell on me. "That's it, Cronin, you're one of our witnesses next Tuesday. Get yourself ready."

GULP!

I knew there already had been tremendous media attention to the hearings which had now garnered the tag "Marcosgate." I had only been working on the case for a few weeks, and I thought to myself, if I mess this one up it is all over. Over the weekend Lorraine pretty much avoided me as I reviewed the countless files and reports in preparation.

Tuesday morning rolled around. I felt that same knot in my stomach the size of a basketball. I walked over to the Foreign Affairs Committee with Chairman Solarz. When I entered the huge room, the knot in my stomach got worse. As I scanned around, there were eighteen television cameras and batteries of microphones at the witness table. In front of that and slightly raised, was the great wood-paneled arc where my inquisitors were arrayed, peering down at me with incredibly serious demeanor.

Guess that if I screwed up I might as well do it in front of the entire nation. Although I had testified on other occasions, it had not been at this level of spectacle. I mentioned to Mike Lewen, the Congressman's Staff Director, that I was nervous — particularly about the cameras and the still photographers. I knew the still photographers would be blasting their flash bulbs as a witness was seated. I was afraid the show would be a terrible distraction for me. Mike patted me on the back and tried to calm me down.

"Relax, it's a piece of cake. The chairman will introduce your testimony as best he can — he's got your back."

With little fanfare, two witnesses preceded me, one was a lawyer, representing one of the principles in the Lindenmere estate who was turning over evidence and the other a lawyer from the committee on Philippine citizens' rights, testifying in support of the committee hearings. As I knew my turn was approaching, I reviewed my notes and records several times. Then I was on. The Chairman identified me as the next witness and I proceeded toward the table. Just as portrayed in the old newsreels it seemed as though I was moving in slow motion. It seemed like an eternity walking up to that large table and sitting there alone before the ten members of the committee.

The fireworks started immediately. Congressman Roth objected to my even being a witness, claiming he had not been notified in advance. He said it was irregular since he had no time to prepare questions for me and did not know the subject of my testimony. Solarz ignored him and proceeded to swear me in. Roth again objected. I was standing between the two as they glared at each other. My right hand was raised but my knees were shaking. Just then in the nick of time, Congressman Pete Toricelli jumped into the argument. As it turned out, the Congress and the General Accounting Office were at that moment engaged in implementing newly passed legislation called the Gramm-Rudman Act. That act gave the Comptroller General broad powers to sequester federal program funds when budget targets were not reached. Toricelli referenced the Gramm-Rudman act by stating that if this man is from GAO we better listen to what he has to say since under the new law, the GAO is now running the Federal Government.

Then it was Roth and Toricelli's turn to tangle. A red-faced Roth loudly objected to Toricelli's statement saying it was totally irrelevant to the proceeding. Solarz again intervened and got things back on track, chastising Roth for objecting and reminding him of his own prior statements about the lack of evidence.

"You have constantly said there was no evidence," Solarz said. "Well, we now have a man in front of us who is going to present the evidence and you don't want him to be heard?" Then the Chairman just looked at me and in a loud voice shouted, "Mr. Cronin, raise your right hand!"

I was sworn in, somehow found the chair, and sat down. I grabbed for the pitcher and the water glass and took a large drink. At that point I needed the drink of water and that seat very badly.

A double martini might have been better.

Solarz then began to lead me through a series of questions. First, he had me introduce the tax records and explain them and their relation to the various corporate entities and the offshore bank accounts. He next had me review the four demand letters asking for payment for the work done rehabilitating the Lindenmere Estate. The third line of questioning centered on my struggles to obtain information from the Commerce Department on the filings of the seven corporations.

Just before we went into the hearings, the General Counsel of the Commerce Department had informed me that four of the companies had not filed the required reports and three had. He said they would only provide me with summary information—no details. At least that was a step in the right direction. Solarz had asked House Counsel for a ruling on whether the Department was required to provide us with the names. It was his opinion that it was, but for the moment we were stonewalled.

I remember after the hearing was over remarking to Mike Lewen how I was glad the photographers didn't take too many pictures to distract me. He laughed and said although I never noticed, the flash bulbs were popping all over the place while I was being sworn in, as well as during the testimony.

Sometimes being a little paralyzed is a good thing.

That evening with my wife and two boys, we stayed glued to the television, switching back and forth from channel to channel in order to get the best coverage. My last appearance on national television involved the Donald Duck caper. As previously described, that didn't turn out too well for me. I certainly hoped things would play out better this time. Suddenly there I was, amazingly looking and sounding cool, calm, and collected. I couldn't believe it because I knew what I had felt like inside. For the next few days, GAO associates, neighbors, and friends were all paying compliments about my testimony. I really felt as though I had accomplished something important in a short period of time.

That round of hearings was over, but the inquiry was only beginning. Now it was back to the rest of the Marcos corporations and the thousands of pages of records. In addition to having subpoenaed many of the companies involved in the Marcos transactions, we had now issued subpoenas to a number of New York banks to obtain copies of the pertinent bank account records. As in the case of the property taxes, I was probing through the records looking for inconsistencies or a weak spot. I found the ownership of the estate was covered up nicely through over *twenty* offshore corporations.

I was looking for the "smoking gun", that one mistake that people often make when engaged in illegal or inappropriate activities. Then I hit on a potential area. The records we had obtained from the Security Pacific Bank in California indicated there was a shortfall in the construction account for the renovations of the Herald Center property on Broadway in New York. To avoid a foreclosure on the property by Security Pacific, the owners had to come up with 1.3 million dollars in a very short time frame.

I noticed copies of three certified checks issued by Manufacturers Hanover Trust Company in New York City. Two checks were for 500 thousand dollars and one check for 300 thousand dollars. I quickly arranged for a subpoena to be signed by Chairman Solarz to obtain the pertinent records.

Banks and other financial institutions generally examine subpoenas very carefully—usually for good reason. To avoid "witch hunt" type abuses, most subpoenas are required to be very specific in nature. But when working with wire transfers and other movements of cash, creative alternatives can be developed.

With the assistance of Charles Tiefer, Deputy Counsel for the House of Representatives, we developed some appropriate language. We asked for the specific accounts or documents we knew were in existence and then we added a paragraph that gave a number of the banks heartburn. We asked for any or all books, documents, and records pertaining directly or indirectly to the assets of Ferdinand and Imelda Marcos. That would give me access to all of the records of the bank if I could show any direct or indirect ties to them.

Normally, I would call the banks first and tell them the specific records I wanted and inform them that I had a subpoena. In most cases that was enough, and the banks would cooperate. They would pull the desired records, and with my team I would visit the bank and exchange the subpoena for the records.

It was early in 1986 and I had planned a trip to New York for Monday, January 27 to obtain a number of the bank records I had requested relating to the Bernstein's accounts. On the Friday morning before, I called the Manufacturer Hanover Trust Company to brief them on what I needed in relation to the certified checks. I had copies of the checks in front of me so it should be a simple matter. All I wanted to know was the source of the funds for the three checks. This type of bank record normally could be easily obtained in a few hours. I was connected to a representative of the bank counsel, a gentleman by the name of Mr. Volkimer. I told him it was essential that we have the records by my visit to New York on Monday since we were having another hearing Wednesday.

Futhermore, those records were highly important and that

they could play a vital role in the hearing. I don't think Volkimer realized the importance or the urgency of the investigation. He stated he could not possibly produce the records by Monday. I reminded him of my authority with the Committee, also that as a CPA familiar with bank records, it should not take more than a few hours—and essentially that his position was unacceptable. The Congress of the United States has very broad subpoena power. I decided it was time to use it.

"I will be in New York on Monday and instead of the one subpoena for the records I will be bringing two subpoenas. One is for the records, and I will have a second subpoena requiring the president of Manufacturers Hanover Trust Company to appear before our Subcommittee on Wednesday with the records in hand."

I knew the last thing that a major bank would want was to have their President called before a Congressional Committee. There was a long pause on the telephone.

"Is there any room to negotiate?"

"Like what?"

He responded after another pause. "I think I can have the records by early Monday afternoon."

"Fine. I will see you at one o'clock."

"Oh—and when you come to New York then could you please just bring one subpoena."

I knew which one he did not want me to bring. Actually, it was a bluff. There would not have been sufficient time that day to prepare and process a personal service subpoena for the President of the bank. But thank God Volkimer did not want to take that chance.

I flew to New York Monday morning on the first flight and visited several of the other—more cooperative—banks to pick up copies of the Bernstein accounts that I had requested. Late in

the morning I arrived at the main offices on Park Avenue of Manufacturers Hanover Trust Company. Volkimer had the particular
records in hand.

As I suspected, the certified checks had been funded from
monies in the account of a Glyceria Tantoco, a close associate of
the Marcos' and one of the known go-betweens of Ferdinand and
Imelda Marcos and the Bernstein brothers. Volkimer also handed me a 1.3 million dollar wire transfer message that provided
the trail of funds through the Bankers Trust Fund Company in
New York directly to Manufacturers Hanover Trust. Unfortunately, the document was virtually illegible. Carefully scanning it with
a magnifying glass I saw one word that made my heart jump. It
was "MANILA." I told Volkimer that the illegible copy was non-
responsive to the subpoena. By now he clearly understood that
stonewalling me would not help the situation with the bank. He
promised to find some special equipment to enhance the quality of
the microfilm and have the records for me by that afternoon.

I left the bank to visit the final bank on my list and obtained
their records as I has requested. When I returned a few hours later, a legible copy miraculously had been produced. And there it
was—the closest tie to Marcos yet—a 1.3 million dollar transfer
from the Security Bank and Trust Company of Manila.

A principal owner of the Security Bank was Rolando Gapud
who was known to be a close associate of Ferdinand Marcos *and* the
Marcos' personal banker. One of the officials of a lending bank that
was foreclosing on the Harold Center project was John Getzelman.
Getzelman already had provided us with a sworn affidavit identifying Gapud as having extensive business interests with the Marcos. I
called Congressman Solarz and told him what I had found.

"John, be ready for the cameras again. You are on Wednesday as
the star witness—this is the smoking gun."

That gave me one day to prepare for another major hearing. Remembering all the TV cameras and photographers, I started to get nervous all over again. Wednesday came quickly and suddenly there I was at the table again—unfortunately again only water was in the pitcher. This time, however, fortunately there were no objections from Congressmen Roth and Solomon to my giving testimony.

Solarz opened his hearing by questioning me about the Getzelman affidavit. I went through the details, establishing the significant relationship between Rolando Gapud and Ferdinand Marcos. Then I brought the bomb shell—the closest tie to Ferdinand Marcos yet. I introduced into evidence the wire transfer message and explained how the 1.3 million dollars was obtained. But now Congressman Roth jumped into action. He questioned the validity of the evidence as to how it tied directly to Marcos. I pointed out that I thought the evidence that we had, although circumstantial, was compelling and certainly pointed toward Ferdinand and Imelda Marcos as the ultimate beneficial owners of the properties. Congressman Solarz then went into closing statements. The other panel members' remarks seemed supportive of the case.

Our hearings at this point on what the press had dubbed "Marcosgate" were over. We had established a substantial amount of circumstantial evidence that in fact the Marcos' did own the New York properties. The offshore corporations however provided a secrecy barrier preventing our directly identifying them as the ultimate beneficial owners. I finished my bank analysis work thinking we could do no more. I returned to my more mundane routine of CPA audit quality reviews at the GAO.

Sometimes a little boring can be nice. About six weeks had gone by and suddenly, a major event. Marcos had fled the Philippines to Hawaii. On arrival in Hawaii, the U.S. Customs Service had seized substantial amounts of financial records and valuables. It was an investigators bonanza — and we were back in business. There were bank records, wire transfer records, correspondence, gold, jewels and large sums of currency and several million-dollar certificates of deposit. Congressman Solarz contacted the Commissioner of Customs. An agreement was quickly reached that the customs department would provide copies of all of the records seized from the Marcos plane. Unfortunately, however, the following day Congress took a brief recess. As the Customs Department was preparing to provide copies to Solarz's" committee, attorneys for Ferdinand and Imelda Marcos went to a federal district judge in Hawaii and obtained a restraining order prohibiting the Customs Bureau from turning over the records without an "appropriate subpoena."

Congressman Solarz was furious. Under normal operating rules, Congress does not need to subpoena records from its own federal agencies. They are routinely provided pursuant to request, but the Committee members were all out travelling back to their districts and could not immediately be reached. There now would be a delay of several days before they could vote to issue the subpoenas. Finally the members returned, and the subpoenas were in hand. On March 19th we began reviewing the records.

As luck would have it, early that morning the Comptroller General and I testified before Congress as to our review of the CPA profession and how it relates to the GAO. It was one of the most intense and frustrating periods of my career I can recall — running back and forth between the preparations for the Comptroller General's testimony and the arrangements to review the Marcos records.

I felt like a ten-year-old who had just been given the keys to an ice cream parlor — but whose mother always kept tabs on him.

But the wait for the ice cream was well worth it. The paperwork

I was reviewing went far beyond just the New York properties. The answers to many of the questions that the Bernsteins refused to provide were right before me. We now had a clear indication of the extent to which the Marcos had been stealing. There was a hand-written agreement with Marcos prepared by Joseph Bernstein. It was a declaration of trust on hotel stationary stating that he would establish the various offshore corporations for the benefit of Marcos and his wife. There were numerous certificates of deposits and bankers' acceptances for millions of dollars — all made out to the bearer. There were pages of records indicating kickbacks to Marcos on imports into the Philippines. The standard kickback appeared to be about 15% percent.

Much of the activity centered on imports from the Japanese. There was even a letter from a Japanese official setting forth the specific details of how the payments should be handled. All they wanted was to avoid discovery, even referring to the recent scandal of Prime Minister Tanaka, wishing not to follow in a similar scandalous path. There were receipts from Swiss bank accounts showing the account number and deposits that were made via dummy corporations set up in Hong Kong. The records even demonstrated Mrs. Marcos' affinity for the "lucky" number seven. She always had two or three sevens in her account numbers.

Didn't do her much good though…

The records were so voluminous we had to move them over to space at the subcommittee offices. I briefed Congressman Solarz on the bonanza that had been uncovered. He spent a lot of time going through the records himself. The documentation showed that a President earning about fifty-three hundred dollars a year was stealing well beyond the millions known in New York. In a brilliant move, Solarz had the key records bound and a number of copies made which would be made available to the press for the cost of the printing. The Congressman's idea was to have the entire Washington press corps turn themselves into investigators to uncover the rest of the Marcos wrongdoing.

"Release the hounds!!!"

We were exhausted but there was more. Within a few weeks we had begun working with Philippine Senator Solanga, the Chairman of their commission on good government. He was responsible for overseeing the transition to the new Aquino Government. He and Congressman Solarz called a press conference with the Washington Press corps, tactically held in the same Foreign Affairs Committee room where we had the hearings.

It was a standing room only crowd, replete with the now usual flashbulbs and TV cameras. Several hundred copies of the Congressman's press statement had been printed and placed on the table. In the rush, several members of the press corps fell to the floor and were almost trampled. After the pushing and shoving stopped, Congressman Solarz, along with each of other members of the committee, vied for their space at the microphone.

What a zoo!

Of course each committee member had a prepared statement expressing their outrage on the extent of thievery by the Marcos. Congressman Solarz was very clever with his words.

"Some governments are aristocracies. Some governments are democracies, but the government of Ferdinand and Imelda Marcos was a kleptocracy."

He then turned the microphone over to me for questions from the press corp. As I responded, the cameras again began rolling. Luckily, I was getting pretty good at this as I presented the details of the extent of the stolen millions along with the mundane differences between bankers' acceptances and certificates of deposit and the enormous sums they were worth.

Another exciting day.

I returned home exhausted but energized, pretended to play a bit with the boys, and again dragged the family to the front of the television set. There I was again—live and in color. I was now getting used to seeing myself on national television, not to mention getting to be a regular ham.

The revelations of the degree of plunder of the Philippine people by Ferdinand and Imelda Marcos and the ties to the New York properties turned out to be too much for the Bernsteins. Ralph and Joseph were facing criminal charges. On top of that a contempt citation was passed by the House of Representatives and was forwarded to the United States Attorney. Jail terms for the Bernsteins appeared inevitable. Suddenly the attorneys for the Bernsteins contacted Chairman Solarz. They now wanted to cooperate. A meeting was arranged for the last week in March which actually lasted several days—running from early afternoon to about 9:30 in the evening each day. Chairman Solarz reviewed all the activities and misdeeds of the Bernsteins, but this time they answered all questions fully.

The boys had flipped.

Some of their disclosures were plain shocking. Joseph Bernstein acknowledged having a number of meetings with the Marcos to handle their investments in New York and clearly identified Ferdinand and Imelda Marcos as the ultimate beneficial owners of the properties. He indicated the amount of money available for investment was virtually unlimited. He even described one meeting at the airport where Mrs. Marcos was preparing to leave for a trip to New York to the World Trade Center in support of Philippine export products. President Marcos arrived to see her off. Joseph Bernstein was also present with a large crowd of people seeing off the first lady. Marcos held the departure of the plane for a few moments while he discussed the status of some of his investments with Joseph Bernstein.

In discussing the intimate details of another one of their meetings with the Marcos, Joseph Bernstein described a dinner at the Sign of the Dove Restaurant in New York. Bernstein and others, including the pianist Van Cliburn, were present. During the dinner party, Mrs. Marcos pulled out a Swiss bank account book flashing a balance of 120 million dollars. On another occasion, returning at about midnight to the Sixty-sixth street townhouse, Mrs. Marcos told Bernstein that she wanted to visit her new office building under construction at Forty Wall Street. They re-entered the limousine and along with the exhausted Secret Service protection headed for Wall Street. Once there, Mrs. Marcos stood outside staring up at the building.

"It's the tallest building next to the World Trade Center. Now I am well diversified in New York—up town, down town, east side, west side."

The final chapter in the sad Marcos saga took place on April 9, 1986. The Bernsteins testified in person before the Committee and the collected frenzied media. From our lengthy meetings with the Bernsteins, we had put together a series of box and line charts showing the maze of ownership details of each property through the various offshore corporations. I was asked again to choreograph the hearing. I walked through the specifics of how the corporations were set up and produced additional charts for each of the New York properties. That was my fourth and final television appearance on the matter.

I had mixed feelings about being out of the limelight—but my ego should survive.

Lorraine and I relaxed with my usual martini, with the family enjoying watching my show-stopping performance again that evening on television. My favorite part of the last hearing was that Congressman Roth and Soloman were silent.

Congressman Torecelli asked (on the record) for an apology from them, considering their strong negative comments about the Chairman and members of the Committee. Of course no apology was forthcoming but all of the other members and I shared a heart-felt vindication for our efforts.

19. "Irangate"—Inside Iran-Contra

History yet again repeated itself with another a scandal in the highest offices of the land. The nation's wounds caused by the breakdown in our system from Watergate were healing. I am reminded of a line from a Peter, Paul and Mary song. "When will they ever learn, when will they ever learn." Investigating misdeeds, waste, and fraud in our government is my job, but over time it can be depressing. Good thing I have my crazy Irish sense of humor.

It was a cold blustery day in February 1986 in Washington. The furor over Ferdinand and Imelda Marcos was beginning to die down. I was back at my GAO position continuing to supervise the quality review of the CPA professionals doing business with the government. Being within two to three years of retirement, I was accepting my position to finish out my career as the Director of GAO's Audit Quality Task Force. But as was frequently the case during my career, I was working simultaneously on other projects. In this instance I also had been advising the House Committee on Oversight and Investigations on some matters pertaining to their analysis of government loans.

"No rest for the weary."

Things began to heat up shortly before the Christmas season.

The Iran "arms for hostages" deal scandal broke, along with the possibility of White House involvement. President Reagan had appointed a special board, the Tower Commission, to investigate. Their report was released, and the House and Senate were gearing up their respective investigating committees. When I saw Senator Inouye's name, I remembered my Watergate experiences and said to myself, "Here we go again, another Watergate."

I got another one of those phone calls and was asked to come immediately to Director Fred Wolf's office. Most of my meetings with Fred were open door meetings, sometimes attended by staff. The reports on the CPA profession had shaken things up a lot more than expected, but events were reasonably under control and work was progressing nicely.

I walked in to see Fred, and I immediately sensed the meeting was about more than a status update on the CPA project. He had a funny little smile on his face that worried me a bit. When he went over and shut the door, I knew something serious was about to drop. He told me that he had been in discussions with the Comptroller General. Given that my successful efforts on the Marcos investigation were fairly well known on the Hill, they wanted me to assist the Senate Committee and work as the Chief Accountant on the Iran-Contra probe.

As we have seen, the great majority of GAO's request for work from the Hill originates in the House as opposed to the Senate. The Comptroller General's interest was in supporting these investigations, and using proper protocol, offered GAO audit assistance to the House Committee first. The House Committee however, much preferred to have an investigative team, and requested assistance from GAO's investigations unit. Several investigators were assigned. The House saw no need for auditors or accountants. That shortsighted decision would cause some turmoil later on. The

Senate on the other hand, was quick to perceive the need for accounting support.

After I fulfilled a brief prior commitment to the House Subcommittee on Oversight and Investigations, involving a loss of government funds in the management of the Lake Placid Hotel that had been taken over by the Federal Savings and Loan Insurance Corporation, I was off to meet the Senate Iran-Contra Committee. I left our audit quality wrap up in the hands of my two Deputy Task Force Directors, Leslie Aronovitz who would continue the work in examining how governmental entities procure CPA audits and Dave Clark who would process the report on yet another audit quality issue. Substandard CPA audits of Government loans in the years to follow would become another national mess. Ken Foster, a recently assigned audit manager would oversee the actions taken by the profession on our 57 referrals of CPAs for substandard work.

Beginning in February 1987, my initial contact for the Senate Iran-Contra Committee was with Mark Belnick, the Executive Assistant to their Chief Counsel, Arthur Liman. From that point on, I got to see an awful lot of Arthur and Mark.

As I have discussed before, one of my many frustrations with the various administrations in the conduct of an investigation was obtaining our clearances and access to records. This project was no different. It was as though they wanted an investigation, but just not too deep of one. Early on, Mark Belnick decided to determine if cooperation from the Israeli government could be obtained. This episode shows what we were up against.

After weeks of trying, Belnick had not obtained the required clearance from the Justice Department to make the contact. He drafted a detailed cable for the State Department to send to Israel asking a number of questions on whether Israel would cooperate and provide assistance in the investigation. He prepared the cable at the State Department with assistance from some of their officials. The next step would be for the State Department to rewrite the cable in standard diplomatic language they used when communicating with another country.

Belnick received a phone call from the State Department advising that they had rewritten the cable. Belnick said, "Fine, tell me what it said."

Their answer was, "Sorry, we can't. You are not cleared."

Belnick responded, "But I wrote it."

They said, "We don't care, you're not cleared."

Several weeks later, a response was received at the State Department from Israel. They notified Belnick that the cable had been received. Again, he asked, "What does it say?"

Their response, "We can't tell you, you're not cleared."

Belnick said, "Can't you at least give me the general drift of their response?"

"Alright, they said no."

"*…fun and games with State.*"

Although Arthur Liman and Senator Inouye were told by State that the clearances for the investigative staff would be rushed through in a matter of weeks, that clearly was not happening. Many records containing key information from the Tower Commission had been turned over as well as some records from the Intelligence Oversight Agencies. But none of the investigative staff could have access to any of these records without clearances.

Fortunately, I finally gained access to some of the records. They were obtained from various commercial enterprises in what became known as the "Domestic Network," also sometimes referred to as "The Enterprise."

After reviewing what records I could get my hands on, as well as the Tower Commission report, I discussed with Belnick and Liman an overall plan I had put together for the financial side of the investigation. Given that we were dealing with congressional committees, I had to be sure the plan was relatively simple. We would concentrate our efforts on three major areas: (1) getting the entire story of the Miller-Channel Domestic Fund Raising Network, (2) identifying all the funds involved in the accounts controlled by the Contras, and (3) and obviously the most difficult, obtaining bank and other confidential records or reconstructing them if necessary. We needed to show how the funds passed through what was known as the Enterprise.

It was quickly becoming clear that we would need a fairly good sized, highly capable staff to carry out this complex mission. The Comptroller General was very supportive of this activity. I was given his commitment to provide any additional assistance I needed. This type of blank check is something that happens rarely in the General Accounting Office.

A key senior GAO staff member, Lou Zanardi, had been assigned from our Defense Department area to assist in any work on military equipment sales. Lou was also a CPA, which was a great help. I told the Comptroller General's office that as soon as my detailed plan was finished, we would be needing more staff. For now however, there was still the issue of the damn clearances.

Tempers were beginning to rise with the slowness of the Justice Department in providing clearances for Mark Belnick, myself, and some of the associate counsels.

One thing that astounded me from the beginning was the size of the congressional committees. Everyone, of course, wanted a piece of the publicity pie. With 11 Senators on the one side and 15 Congressmen on the other side, I foresaw a very unwieldy process. Each Senator appointed an associate counsel. That meant 11 associate counsels I had to deal with. Fortunately, with this being such a highly visible investigation, each Senator appointed their associate counsel with great care. I was pleasantly surprised at the qualifications and professionalism of the associate counsels that were appointed. Just about all the counsels arrived within a period of two weeks. We all were crammed into a suite of offices normally held for use by a single U.S. Senator. This was done while a secure facility was being constructed for us in the Hart Senate Office Building.

So we began our work headquartered in the Hart Senate Office Building, often referred to as the Taj Mahal of the Senate. There was much criticism when the building first was constructed about its cost and some of its extra features for entertaining, including a fancy restaurant on the top floor. There was so much denunciation that in fact the restaurant was never completed. The Committee took over the space, and in a period of just four weeks, an entire secure facility was built out. It was an amazing set up.

At the original Senate offices, the problems with the storage of intelligence sensitive documentation were horrendous. Futhermore, there were only two rooms available to us for secure conversations involving very sensitive matters. The Senate Intelligence committee had such a room in the Hart building and also in the Capitol. Often times, the TV cameras were left in place when the Senators and senior staff would use the facility in the Capitol. That was the least desirable of the two until ours was completed. The new space at least would be much more secure from public and media access.

I don't know which frustration was worse — trying to deal with the classified documents in an unsecure, cramped facility, or the on-going difficulties over obtaining clearances. Finally, Arthur Liman and Senator Inouye had had enough. The Senator fired off a letter to the Attorney General citing the numerous delays in my clearance and two others. My case was particularly frustrating since I had been approved for Top Secret material for over 30 years and also had White House and Department of Energy clearances. My case was used as a high-profile example.

The Attorney General was asked by Chairman Inouye to exercise the authority he had to waive individuals into clearance status without the lengthy background investigation. The letter was extremely nasty—even accusing the Attorney General of slowing down the Congressional investigating process for political purposes.

His letter went out on a Monday morning. Wednesday, at 10:00 p.m., the Justice Department granted our clearances. I remember it well. When dealing with intelligence clearances, they are called Sensitive Compartmented Information, or SCI for short. The other popular term was "code word" clearances. Since the focus of our investigation involved the National Security Agency, the National Security Council, and the Central Intelligence Agency, we had to be granted a lot more than the usual number of clearances. Once those clearances are granted, usually each affected agency has a security briefing. And that's finally what we had.

There was a total of about eight of us attending, five who had been cleared by investigation and the three of us that had been waved in directly by the Attorney General. The security briefing from the agencies only took about two-and-one-half hours, and was held in a secure, steel-lined, briefing room at the Justice Department. Some portions of the briefings were absolutely ridiculous. For example, at one point they showed us a film of a U-2 reconnaissance aircraft. The film was labeled "Top Secret." What was frustrating about this is that the U-2 had long since been replaced by the SR-71 "Blackbird." My small son several years earlier had obtained a detailed scaled model of the SR-71 and built it from a kit. The kit contained all the detailed operational statistics of the aircraft.

Most of the rest of the briefings were about the need to protect classified documents. This too seemed a bit silly since we all had dealt with classified documents for years. This was particularly irritating since many of us already were putting in 12 plus hour days plus weekend work.

"Federal bureaucracy at its finest."

At least the move to our new offices went quickly. One day cramped in old offices in Hart, the next morning fully set up in the new facility on the top floor. The move went without a hitch and the investigation continued without any loss of time.

Now to implement my plans for the financial side of the investigation. Figuring out the domestic fund-raising network would be handled by Lou Zanardi, but I could see we needed some powerful computer facilities for the extensive analysis that would be required. I put in a request for computer expert and former staff member, Chris Martin. Chris was a brilliant young CPA, who was very capable in the design and use of computer systems for audit and investigative purposes, was assigned. Seeing that many of the records we had obtained from the Contras were in Spanish, I asked for two Spanish speaking auditors. In a matter of days after Martin was assigned, we got Olga Johnson and Janet Mixner, both of whom were fluent in Spanish. Another very capable staff member assigned to help with the identification of the financial network was Robin Wagner. My team complete, we began the financial investigation of the Iran-Contra scandal, now being referred to in the press as "Irangate."

It is not my intent here to go over all the grinding details of the investigation—of who did what to whom, or more specifically "what did you know and when did you know it?" We joked that with some background music it could become a theme song for the TV series about the investigation.

The accounting side of probes like this often get set aside in the shadows because without proper training, complex financial transactions are difficult for many people to understand. I think it is important to examine and report what we found in simple terms so that the many officials who supported the Contra movement can understand how they were taken to the cleaners. In this way the average person can understand how it always is a mistake to privatize foreign policy and to put it in the hands of what I called "the gang who couldn't shoot straight."

While none of the three main prongs of our inquiry could be considered easy, the detailing of the "Miller Channel" fundraising network was probably the most straightforward. Not so much from the sense of the work involved, but easier in a sense of our gaining access to the appropriate materials. All of these were domestic activities, the records of which could be obtained by Senate subpoena. The Miller-Channel network raised 10.4 million dollars in support of the Contras. Senator Rudman described their fund-raising effort as the old one two pitch. Colonel Oliver North would give a presentation on the need to "support" the Contras. He would leave the meeting and the others would lay out the detailed needs for weapons and the other supplies.

Our activities unfortunately were frequently interrupted and had to take a back seat to all the media hoopla over who knew what and when. The bottom line of our analysis was simple. Out of the $10.4 million raised by Miller-Channel, the contras only received $1.5 directly. $7.2 million was retained by six Miller-Channel organizations under the umbrella of an entity called the National Endowment for the Preservation of Liberty—a subsidiary of the

Enterprise. The funds were "retained for expenses." The contributors were provided with tax deductions since NEPL was a tax-exempt organization. The difference of $1.7 million went to Colonel North's minions, Albert Hakim and General Richard Secord to their famous Swiss bank accounts. Very little of the money ever got to the Contras, as will be detailed later.

Interestingly, one of the contributors, a Ms. Ellen Garwood, contributed $1.6 million after a special plea made by Colonel North, complete with tears in his eyes about the needs of the Contras. Ironically, had Ms. Garwood given her money directly to the Contras, they would have received 100 thousand dollars more than the *total* they received from the $10.4 million collected by Miller-Channel. Because of our scrutiny and audits, Miller and Channel pled guilty to violations of income tax laws since they had taken from donors "tax deductible contributions" that were not in fact used for tax exempt purposes. So much for the domestic part of our examination, except that it is my hope that those people who contributed will have a sense of feeling that they were "ripped off" and know better in the future.

By now Chris Martin had designed a sophisticated computer model for tracing all the transactions of the Enterprise and their related bank accounts. We began with the accounts of Aldolfo Calero, one of the principle leaders of the Contras. It was a good starting point because at least Calero and the Contras had cooperated by providing copies of their bank statements, canceled checks, and related financial documents. They included several items called "offshore" accounts that were located in Panama and the Cayman Islands. My staff examined every transaction and input everything we knew about each document into the system. We were tracking both transferring and receiving banks, trying to get a handle on the flow of monies. After the Marcos investigation, I certainly was pretty familiar with the goings on of these offshore "banks." Early in our analysis of the Contra accounts we saw many transactions involving a number of banks in the Miami area and one bank in New Orleans. Based on that information, I organized what I called the "Miami Sweep." Five of us, including an investigator from the House Iran/Contra Committee, prepared to head South.

I left a day early to travel by way of New Orleans in order to make a stop at that particular bank—which happened to be near the airport. We had alerted the bank as to my visit. Despite that, when I arrived, I was greeted by a young woman Vice President who appeared quite nervous. When I handed her the subpoena and she handed me the records, I could see why. The account was opened by Mario Calero, Aldolfo's brother. Most of the people involved in the operation were trying to keep it secret but it seems Mario Calero was not very good at that. In fact, he put the logo of the Nicaraguan Resistance right on the checks themselves, along with their full name. When I later showed these checks to Adolfo Calero, he just shook his head and moaned about his brother's stupidity. This one account showed the sources of funds coming from various Swiss bank accounts. It was used to support the Contras for purchases of uniforms and other equipment. It also conveniently identified some of the suppliers.

The next day we executed a similar operation in Miami. We split up into teams and visited the particular banks armed with our subpoenas. We obtained the accounts and returned to the hotel. Analysis of these accounts yielded even more funds in other banks. After three days, we returned to Washington with the equivalent of a foot-locker full of bank records.

Most bankers fully cooperate with a congressional or a law enforcement investigation. They just want to avoid any violation of bank secrecy laws and need their actions to be covered by a subpoena. But as was the case in the Marcos investigation, there always seems to be one who wants to resist. Usually, it is the bank legal department that tries to put up the roadblocks. At times I must conclude that there must be a special place in hell for some lawyers. This time the obfuscating bank was the Greater Southeast Bank, one of the largest banks in Miami.

During the Marcos investigation, I developed subpoena language strong enough to access any relevant documents in a bank, not just the accounts themselves. This is necessary in order to be able to fully trace wire transfers. If the subpoena would only ask for a particular account or a group of transactions in the account, and we found a reference to another account within the same bank, standard subpoena language would not let us trace to that account. Time then would be needlessly lost getting another subpoena.

Of course none of the banks were especially fond of the broad language of my subpoena, but the lawyers at Greater Southeastern took particular exception. I advised them that it was within our authority. Unfortunately, to make it plain and simple — we got stonewalled. After several visits and lengthy discussions, they still failed to produce the records. I advised the bank that on my return to Washington I would issue a personal service subpoena for the President of the bank to come to Washington with the records I had requested in hand, and personally present them to the Committee in a formal deposition. I guess we left on some very unfriendly terms.

In sensitive investigations such as these, total support from my top management is an absolute must. In this situation we had that support. In this particular case, it was Mark Belnick who came to my aid. I had told Mark about the difficulties with Greater Southeast. I had hardly finished discussing the issues with him when a call came in for Mark from one of the bank's Vice Presidents. He was irate and told Belnick that he objected to my requests as being too broad and that I was "using strong arm tactics." I was in the room during the conversation. Belnick fired back at the vice president, "That's exactly why we hired Mr. Cronin."

Belnick continued, "You have a choice, you can give Mr. Cronin the records he wants, or you can refuse, and as he told you, you will be served by the U.S. Marshals and you and your President can come here to Washington and talk to 11 very unhappy Senators."

There was silence from the other end of the phone for a full minute. Then the Vice President cleared his throat and told Belnick that there was probably a terrible misunderstanding and that he would like me to call him as soon as possible. Belnick slammed down the phone.

"Go get them, John."

A few moments later I called the banker back. He advised that they had located the records I had asked for, and they were being sent to me in the overnight mail. They also said they hoped this would clear things up so as not to have their president subpoenaed to come to Washington. I agreed to their request, chuckling to myself as I did. None of us really had any intention of taking the time and effort to send U.S. Marshalls to bring the banker to Washington.

Gradually entries were building up in our data base. We even were beginning to reconstruct the Swiss account known as "Lake Resources" from the records we had obtained from the Contras and those subpoenaed from the many banks and suppliers. It was a slow, tedious process, but our big breakthrough was yet to come.

Albert Hakim had agreed to provide us with the records from the Enterprise as the quid pro quo for an immunity order issued by the Committee. Hakim was the individual who kept the books of the Enterprise and was directly involved with most of the arms deal negotiations. There were many Congressional objections and questions about giving immunity to him and Oliver North. But had we not, in my opinion the whole Iran-Contra story would never have been revealed.

Negotiations were underway with Hakim's lawyer to have a deposition in Paris, on neutral ground where we could also obtain the documents and records he held. While we were waiting for word on the final negotiation with Hakim, another development would help us.

We had been trying to obtain information on an offshore bank in the Cayman Islands in connection with a number of transactions, including some of the infamous Oliver North travelers check transactions. The intelligence and law enforcement services of a friendly foreign government—the United Kingdom—came to our aid. We were informed that one of the Cayman Island banks we had been watching was in reality just a mail drop with a Cayman Island address. The individual accounts were actually maintained in a Miami bank. We had visited that Miami bank, and it was clear that the bank officers had lied to us. Since it is a criminal violation to lie to federal investigators, the Justice Department would become involved. Over the years of prior investigations, we had a great working relationship with the Justice Department and the Bureau of Customs. Both gave us quite a bit of help and support. Now I was in a position to return the favor.

GAO's primary investigation was only interested in one of the four thousand accounts I had uncovered. Since some people use offshore accounts for various types of questionable or illegal activities, a call to the Justice Department was in order. I notified them of our findings. We visited the bank with our subpoena and obtained the Iran-Contra records we needed. Immediately after we walked out the door, the other law enforcement agencies raided the bank and seized the records for the other four thousand accounts.

Interestingly enough, but typical for this type of operation, all this bank possessed were transaction tapes. They recorded the deposits and checks and sent the summary tapes to a bank in Costa Rica for processing. Since all the transactions were recorded in a bank in the U.S., they were easily accessed by subpoena, both ours and the law enforcement agencies.

You may be asking, what is the name of the bank? I have deliberately not identified the bank involved in this part of the transaction. But for those involved, I hope this creates a little insecurity for them—and for that matter, anyone thinking of using offshore banks for criminal activity.

By now it was the week before Easter, and we were still waiting for word on the final agreements with Hakim. We were tentatively scheduled on the 6 o'clock flight Easter Sunday from Washington to Paris. We knew that the remaining details would not be worked until the last minute. John Neilds, the House Counsel, would be in charge of the hearing. It would be conducted by Senator McClure and Congressman Chaney who were already in Europe. It was arranged that Senator Inouye and Congressman Hamilton would be in touch by speaker phone which would be middle of the night Washington time. Kip Holmes, one of our Associate Counsels would be the senior representative of the Senate committee. George Van Cleve, the chief minority counsel of the House, also attended. Oh, and I got to tag along as Chief Accountant.

Even as we packed our paperwork and left the office on Saturday, the trip was still not finalized. The last-minute plan was that everyone would go to Dulles airport except me. Since I lived only a short distance away, I would stay by my telephone waiting for the decision. In connection with this investigation, we were not able to tell anyone about our ongoing work or our pending travel. Lorraine had invited the family for Easter dinner. My bags were packed and waiting in the car. At 4 o'clock some of the family members arrived and Easter festivities started. I sat near the phone with my martini. A little before five Arthur Liman called and said that the meeting was a go. Making my apologies to everyone, I headed for the airport, parked my car, and entered the terminal. Five anxious faces were awaiting me and the word that the trip was on. We headed for the plane and left at 6 o'clock. We arrived at Orly airport at 7 a.m.

Not that sleeping on a plane is ever easy, no one got much rest given the anticipated excitement of the day. The plan was that Hakim, after being given the immunity order, and answering questions that had been previously supplied to his lawyer, he would turn over the records and all relevant documents. It was anticipated that he would have kept the records in Switzerland and once he was given the immunity order he would have them flown to Paris. I and designated staff members would stay in Paris to review the records and determine that we had been given what was promised.

Easter Monday is a holiday in France and the streets of Paris were deserted. The State Department limo took us to the offices of Paul Reiss Rifkin, the firm that had employed Arthur Liman and Mark Belnick. This was one of the terms required by Hakim's attorney. They were concerned that if the hearing was held on U.S. soil at the U.S. Embassy, Hakim could be arrested. Probably a wise precaution. Hakim arrived 10 minutes before the scheduled hearing. He was a small man, with mid- eastern features, trying to smile and be as polite as possible. The hearing started.

Hakim was asked the series of prearranged questions by John Neilds, House Committee Counsel, which he refused to answer based on his Fifth Amendment constitutional rights. At that point, Senator Inouye and Chairman Hamilton were present on the speaker phone. It was about three in the morning in Washington. Over the phone, both chairmen read Hakim the immunity order he was waiting for, and then the questioning resumed. He began by answering some basic questions about his operation of the Enterprise and the extent of the receipts and disbursements that passed through his hands. He was again read the section of the immunity order pertaining to the records and he agreed that they would be produced. To our amazement, when the hearing was concluded, Hakim announced the records were actually in Paris and they would arrive within 10 minutes of a phone call. The call quickly was made and shortly thereafter the records arrived.

It was an exciting moment. Armed guards brought them in a gigantic duffel bag at least the size of a body bag. The records had been arranged nicely in a series of loose leaf binders. Lou Zanardi and I began going through the documents. It didn't take long to confirm that we had exactly the records we needed. We saw documents pertaining to a number of transactions we knew about and saw that we had a reasonably complete set of ledgers and bank records. We immediately telephoned Arthur Liman to let him know that we had the records. Not knowing what would happen when we arrived at the meeting site in a State Department vehicle, we had left our luggage in the van. Now with the records in hand, we saw no need to stay in Paris. We asked when the next flight left. That flight left in about an hour. We were to leave on the same plane we flew in on.

"Quick trip — huge results!"

The State Department worked quickly. We got back in the van and en route back to the airport, arrangements were made for our seats on the plane. Of course, given the nature of our visit, we had the full cooperation of United States and French security forces.

When we had arrived in France, we went straight from the plane to an awaiting van without going through immigration. Upon our return however, as we were escorted through the airport and to the waiting aircraft, French security got a bit concerned about this large body bag we were carrying with us. A quick meeting between their security people and ours got that problem resolved. Someone suggested we check it as luggage. I told them, "no way"—those records were staying right with us in the cabin. We momentarily joked, "Can you imagine after all this, to have the Swiss records turn up as lost baggage." We arrived at Dulles airport at about 4 p.m. Monday, Washington time. Twenty-two hours after our original departure.

Lorraine was shocked to see me arriving home. She knew I had left the country but did not know my destination. When I told her that I had been to Paris, she looked at me in doubt. I handed her a bottle of perfume I had bought at the duty-free shop during the few moments we had just before we got on the plane. That more than convinced her.

There is no need to bore the reader by going through a detailed presentation here of what we found and all the different expenditures. The bottom line was the Enterprise had taken in a total of $48 million from various sources. The majority of the cash came from the arms sale to Iran. More than $36 million again was the actual cost of the weapons sold to Iran. Ultimately the Contras came up short $12.2 million. The rest of the revenues went into the pockets of Clines, Hakim, and Secord as "residuals"—not to mention what had been set aside for North.

Other expenditures were made for a number of "related" projects including the special intelligence activities that North had supported under the CIA Director Casey. Most of the $12 million had been earmarked for the principals of the Enterprise, including

Oliver North. Fortunately, the money was located, frozen by the courts, and was in litigation for a long, long time as the rightful owners are discerned.

Our analysis of the accounting records disclosed the sale of thousands of weapons, ammunition, and other military gear. The profiteering by the arms dealers was of course also enormous, however it was not our duty to report on that. The Enterprise was powerful in protecting its high profits which ranged from 40 to 155 percent of the cost of the arms sold to the Contras. It was actually pretty amazing they could come up with so much money.

One particular incident shows the cut-throat nature of North, Hakim, and Secord. A retired Major General John K. Singlaub was independently very active in supporting the Contras. He had obtained a secure source of good weapons in China and was selling the weapons to the Contras for about half of the prices that the Enterprise was charging. Calero was informed by Oliver North to stop doing business with Singlaub if they wanted to receive the continued support of the United States government and the Enterprise. Calaro told us he reluctantly had to agree.

Meanwhile our drudgework continued. By now, the seven-day weeks and twelve hour days were taking their toll. My entire team was exhausted. Then came the announcement. The House and Senate Committees investigating would be merged into a single Committee for the hearings. There was much discussion on how to handle the witnesses with 26 Senators and Congressmen doing the questioning. Everyone knew it would be difficult but to have witnesses appear before two committees would be worse.

There was extensive discussion between Senator Inouye, Congressman Hamilton, Arthur Liman, and John Neilds as they all jockeyed for the political spotlight. Neither side gave in, so a decision was made to split up the witnesses. Each Committee would be responsible for certain witnesses. Ironically the House Committee drew Albert Hakim which meant the money story. Suddenly, they realized the money story was far bigger and more complex than they had ever envisioned. It was obvious now that they regretted their decision not to accept the Comptroller General's earlier offer to provide accountants to help.

Since the committees were now "merged," Arthur Liman told me to make all of our accounting data available to the House Committee. More extra work for us. By this time Chris Martin and the staff had amassed an enormous database on our new, sophisticated computers. We briefed John Neilds and members of his key House staff on what we had. Since they had no accountants, they hired the accounting firm of Price Waterhouse. Fortunately, from my work within the profession, I knew the partner-in-charge Ed Haller, fairly well. Unfortunately, it was now clearer than ever. The duplication and repetition was killing us. There should have never been two separate committees in the first place.

But of course, politics rule. I now had to please 11 Senators and 15 Congressmen on two committees plus their massive supportive staffs. Totally unwieldy. It would have been so much easier to handle this as a joint committee with fewer members—as it was done during the Watergate investigation. It is truly a pity we do not learn from history.

The individual committee staffs split up the witnesses as to House witnesses and Senate witnesses. That was the easy part. Since Hakim was to be a House witness, I gave all the material we had developed on the Enterprise to be used for questioning Hakim to Ed Haller and his staff. We gave them much of the data in summary form but kept our three computers humming to cross reference and reconcile all the details with the overall financial statements to be used during the hearings.

Somehow, we managed to pull it off. On some of the evenings before a hearing, we would be going over the final numbers until midnight. But all the work was worth it. The detailed schedules were there and the full financial story on the Enterprise was made public. It was such a convoluted scenario of companies and off-shore corporations that I am sure it confused most of the American people. One conclusion, however, is totally clear. In the course of this whole operation the American public was duped, the Contras were conned, and even the Grand Ayatollah helped fund this group's operation.

21. "Irangate"—The Conclusion

There was still one link in the financial structure remaining un-accounted for—a missing ten million dollars. We had learned during the investigation that the State Department had solicited a $10 million contribution to the Contras, directly from the Sultan of Brunei. Oliver North had provided Assistant Secretary of State Elliot Abrams with the Enterprise bank account number to handle the deposit. Somehow, two of the first three digits became transposed. Belnick came back from a meeting at the State Department and showed me two documents and asked if I knew what they were. I recognized them as wire transfer messages being sent to a New York Bank. He and Arthur Liman asked me if I could use that to trace the $10 million. I told them I could, but I would have to go to New York.

Liman retorted, "Go to New York, go to Switzerland, go to Brunei, go anywhere you have to go in this world, but find that damn money."

In reviewing the documents more closely, something didn't register correctly. Something was wrong—then it hit me. I had been living with the Lake Resources account number for several months. Lake was another name used by the Enterprise to help cover their tracks. Something was wrong with the number on the document. I cross checked it against some of the other documents and spotted the transposition. The correct number of the Lake Resources account was 386-430-22-1, but these wire transfer documents had the account 368-430-22-1. Now I assumed it was just a matter of tracing that wrong number through the New York and Swiss Bank systems.

Little did I know what was in store for me. I sent a copy of the wire messages to the New York banks, namely Citibank and Credit Suisse. I told them I would be visiting them with a subpoena and needed all relevant bank records pertaining to the transaction. I also asked both banks to have any additional information on hand that could shed light on the transfers from their overseas branches to help explain what had happened in the accounts.

Coincidently, when I arrived in New York I served the subpoena on John Redding, the same Citibank official I had served during the Marcos investigation. I got that "look" and comment, "Oh, you again." This time luckily things went smoother. They now were familiar with my subpoena language and knew exactly what I wanted.

Getting me the information from Switzerland however was a different story. After several meetings with Redding and John Duffy, a vice-president of Credit Suisse, plus discussions by telephone with various Swiss officials, there was suddenly concern that the money may have been stolen. The most recent document that had been sent back to Credit Suisse in New York was a wire transfer message originated by a bank employee that senior bank officials in Switzerland had never heard of.

So, it was off to Switzerland for some more excitement—as soon as I could return to Washington to pick up some tickets. The concern over the potential theft, as well as the multiple accesses I had to intelligence information, led Senator Inouye to conclude that I should not make the trip alone and unprotected. I was assigned a security person to accompany me and an additional one in Switzerland. It was certainly a different experience for a GAO auditor/investigator. Pretty heady stuff. I had never traveled with people with guns whose sole purpose was to keep me alive or from being kidnaped. At least Lorraine was pleased.

"Who says accountants never have any fun?"

I was off to Switzerland. I had made arrangements to talk to the Citibank manager in Zurich, a Gordon Insley, and the Credit Suisse manager in Geneva by the name of Mr. Pasa.

I still was not used to the long plane ride, so I began to strike up a fast friendship with the security person assigned. It turned out that he was the Chief of the Capitol Hill Police Department, Jim Carvino. He had an interesting background which made it easy for us to hit it off. He also was raised in New York and spent his first career in the New York City Police Department, eventually becoming the head of the narcotics division. On retirement he moved to Racine, Wisconsin as Chief of Police, and then on to Capitol Hill. Over the course of the trip, Jim and I would swap many stories on our investigative experiences. Jim's were quite a bit more interesting because he was frequently getting shot at.

As a Capitol Hill policeman drove us to the airport, I received a "priority" phone call from the Department of State. I was aware there is a procedure used when investigators such as myself traveled in a foreign country. State obtains what they call "host country clearance," but the Swiss had just communicated some concerns about my visit.

Normally when banks overseas are visited by law enforcement officials, arrangements are covered through a special pact we have with most governments called the Mutual Legal Assistance Treaty.

It operates as a government to government operating blueprint between the respective law enforcement agencies. The issue was apparently that I was not representing a law enforcement agency but acting on behalf of the United States Senate. I already had answered some cables from Switzerland as to the purpose of my visit and there were several telephone calls between the State Department and Swiss officials.

The State Department even suggested that I might not go. We were still talking on the car telephone, sitting outside the terminal at National Airport. With all the pressures on me, I had just about had it with the feet dragging at the State Department. I told them they had better get moving as fast as they could because I had a job to do and was going to get on that plane. If necessary, we were leaving without host country clearance and that I would be pleased to meet with the Swiss government officials on my arrival. I suggested that if they were really concerned, they could intercept me when the plane landed in Zurich prior to the last hop to Geneva.

We flew up to New York and boarded a 747 for Zurich and Geneva. Even back then, airlines get a little nervous when people travel with security. Pan-Am asked us if we had any preferences as to where we sat. We indicated no, but since I was well over six feet, I wanted some leg room for the long flight. But Pan Am came through, partly I'm sure due to security reasons. They put us on the upper deck of the 747 all by ourselves since the flight was somewhat empty. The only disadvantage was we could not see the movie. Not being movie-goers we did not care anyway, plus we had plenty to go over regarding the upcoming meetings. So, we had our own little comfortable conference room and our own cabin attendant on the upper deck.

When we arrived in Geneva, we were greeted as we got off the plane by a State Department security officer by the name of

George Kralis. We would get to know George well during our 10 day stay in Geneva. George provided us with the Swiss accounting documents for our stay and provided Carvino with a Swiss permit for his pistol. With George's security clearances we were quickly ushered through the airport immigration and customs system into a waiting Daimler that took us to our hotel.

Along the way, George handed me a note he had just received from the Swiss government. It put everything on hold. It was quite an official diplomatic note, submitted in French, with a translation attached for my benefit.

"The Federal Police Office of the Federal Justice and Police Department presents its compliments to the embassy of the United States of America in Bern having knowledge, and its note dated May 5th, 1987. It furthermore refers to the telephone conversation of the same date with Mr. Alan Reingold, legal attache' at the U.S. embassy and states that a decision regarding the approval of the requested authorization can be made only at the end of the investigation procedure now being made by this office, i.e. after receiving the advice of all persons and authorities concerned.

Until such date Mr. Cronin will not be in a position to take any official step without infringing the provision of article 271 of the Swiss penal code. The Federal Police Office of the Federal Justice and Police Department will keep the embassy of the United States informed of further steps being taken in regard to its request and endows itself of this opportunity to renew the insurance of its high esteem."

Well, the contrived note made no sense, but actually meant that if I went near a bank I would be arrested. Futhermore, I was advised that I would be under surveillance by Swiss security personnel to make sure that I behaved. We were tired since we had flown all night and it was now mid-morning. Nevertheless, we took the opportunity to make some phone calls. A meeting quickly was arranged for the next day with the Swiss office of Federal Police. We needed to get to the bottom of this delay as soon as possible.

The next morning, reasonably rested but still suffering some jet lag, we headed for Bern in a limousine provided by the State Department. I sensed the situation may have improved. I was suddenly not just a government traveler, traveling as a supervised second-class citizen—I was receiving the treatment reserved for a visiting ambassador. I must confess, the latter was more enjoyable.

The trip to Bern was uneventful except driving down the highways at speeds approaching 100 mph was a little unnerving. I continued rehearsing my little speech to the Swiss. I planned to take a position that I was not in Switzerland to conduct an investigation but merely to obtain clarification of documentation I had already legally obtained in the United States.

The meeting was scheduled for 11 o'clock and we arrived nearly on time. A senior official from the U.S. embassy, George Henderson, was waiting for us. Before proceeding into the meeting, Henderson complained with some displeasure about my visit to Switzerland without having first obtained full host country clearance. I gave him a nasty look and said, "Let's get this meeting started."

We were ushered into a large conference room beautifully paneled with a massive antique inlaid twenty-five foot long conference table. Eight Swiss officials were lined up on one side of the table. Their group was headed by a Doctor Frye, a senior official of their Justice Department. Everyone was introduced with the appropriate formalities exchanged. Each presented the compliments to the other side—then it was my turn up to bat.

I explained in detail the purpose of our investigation and my visit. I clarified all the work that I did in the New York banks and that many of the records pertaining to this transaction, in fact all of them, had been transmitted by them to New York by fax machine. I further made clear that I was not there to conduct an investigation but merely to meet with the bankers and get some clarifications of various codes and explanations of the documents I had already, so I could better understand exactly what happened to the money.

I may have complicated matters a little bit for the Swiss by trying to explain that I had a dual function. I showed them a cable from the Sultan of Brunei's bank that clearly authorized me to represent him in finding out what had happened to his money. Dr. Frye asked if he could see the documents that I had obtained. I thought for a moment and figured it was time for a gamble.

As everyone knows, the Swiss are very proud and protective of their banking system. I thought I would express similar concerns in regard to protecting documents obtained in the United States in response to a Senate subpoena. On that basis I then refused to show Dr. Frye the documents. I knew I was getting somewhere when I saw the reaction on their faces. Then I said I didn't want to stop the discussions. I knew they had the full legal authority to obtain those documents in Switzerland directly from the banks. They just had no authority to obtain them from me. I suggested that as a compromise, we could use the telephone in the room and conference call their bank officials. If we could get an authorization, then I would release my records to them.

Amazingly, then we had a big breakthrough. Dr. Frye concurred and we all moved to the end of the conference room where there was a small table with a telephone. The Swiss pride themselves on the quality of all their products. Their watches are certainly well known for the highest standards, their trains run on time, in fact you can set your Swiss watch by them. And their electronics are equally well made except for this one telephone in the conference room. It would not work. Dr. Frye became quite disturbed and kept constantly depressing the switch hook trying to get an outside telephone line. I may have made matters worse with a comment by saying, "Don't worry about that, Dr. Frye, that happens in the United States every once in a while, too."

He fired back, "Well, it shouldn't happen here in Switzerland."

Matters deteriorated more when I said, "Do you think we can go somewhere and find a phone that works?" He dispatched one of his lawyers, a Mr. Gaussant, to go with me to locate another phone. Gaussant and I left the meeting. We left the Swiss on one side of the table and the remainder of the U.S. delegation staring at each other across the table.

We went down the hall to Gaussant's office and were able to contact the bankers by phone. One of the bankers' secretaries told Gaussant that her boss was too busy to come to the phone. Gaussant began speaking in French—he was very agitated. I understood just enough French to know that he had just threatened her boss with arrest if he did not get on the phone. Suddenly, the banker was on the phone and the clearances obtained.

When I returned to the meeting, I'm not sure why, but I made another seemingly odd choice. Rather than have the two countries on opposite sides of the table, I left the U.S. delegation and walked around the long table to the Swiss side. I asked Dr. Frye if he would move aside to let me sit next to him and between some of their other officials. With that done, I produced all the records I had and explained the details of the flow of the transactions from Brunei through New York and ultimately to the Swiss banks. I showed them that despite some of the transfer messages being hard to read because of the quality of the fax, more than enough of the pertinent information was there.

However, all the Swiss in the room were police officials and lawyers. There were no accountants, and worse, of course I did not have all the documents. If I had all the documents pertaining to the transaction, I would have known where the money was. However, I was able to end the meeting with the implication that indeed I had all the documents. The meeting was concluded, and I got an indication from Dr. Frye that they would move quickly and soon would probably have a favorable reaction to my request to visit the banks.

After the meeting, Henderson and I took the limo over to the U.S. Embassy where I met with our Ambassador, Faith Whittlesey. She was somewhat distracted since at that time she was having a bit of her own difficulties with some unrelated audits and investigations that will not be detailed here. I explained the purpose of my visit and she promised to assist in any way she could. I asked her to contact both the Swiss Foreign Minister and the Justice Minister to see if they could expedite the decision, which she did.

By this time, it was early afternoon, and we were ready for a late lunch. The driver selected a delightful little German restaurant since Bern was in the German section of Switzerland. Our embassy had given me a daily food allowance of four Swiss francs — comparable to that which visiting Senators received. Feeling flush, I bought lunch for George, Jim, and the driver, who kept his Uzi in a grey cloth bag on the seat next to him. After lunch, we had a more leisurely drive back to Geneva, or maybe I was getting used to driving at those European speeds. At any rate the wiener-schnitzel sat well.

I look on that day as a great breakthrough. But that said, the long seven-day work weeks again were taking their toll. Carry-out, fast food, plus the occasional five-star extravaganza dinners had caused me to gain over 25 pounds during this investigation. Arriving at the hotel late every evening and snacking didn't help either—I was gaining weight at leaps and bounds. In fact, my weight had crept up to 225 pounds.

While waiting for approval of my request to visit the banks, I will always remember one particular food-laden day. Early that morning, Jim and I ate breakfast since it was included at the hotel restaurant where we were staying. It had a beautiful view of Lake Geneva. I normally do not eat breakfast, but since it was included, Jim and I had a nice omelet and a croissant for breakfast and several cups of tea while waiting for our limousine. For our lunch I could not resist the good German food. So, I had another wiener-schnitzel with fried potatoes. Finally, as we were getting to know George Kralis quite well, he indicated that he would stay for dinner with us. George suggested a nice restaurant in old town Geneva that made the best fondue in Switzerland. It was indeed the best fondue I had ever eaten. No wonder when this was over, in addition to my weight problem, my cholesterol level had skyrocketed.

Lorraine and my doctor were not pleased.

The next day was Friday, another slow day of waiting. Jim and I worked from the U.S. mission in Geneva, most of the time on the telephone with Henderson in Bern arranging for the clearances to visit the banks. At one point I got a little short with Henderson upon learning that the order for me to go into the banks was in the Justice Minister's inbox awaiting signature. I asked him to have the Ambassador call the Justice Minister and get the order signed. He tried to intimidate me.

"Calling the Justice Minister is like you calling your Attorney General directly and you wouldn't do that, would you, Mr. Cronin?"

I fired back, "No, I wouldn't—I would call Senator Inouye and have him call the President and have him order the Attorney General to sign the damn thing."

Henderson said, "Don't get excited. I'll see what I can do." By late afternoon Friday it was a go.

But naturally there was one more twist. Before I had left New York, officials of both Citibank and Credit Suisse had agreed to talk in person with me. Suddenly, on learning of the involvement of the Swiss government, Credit Suisse withdrew its approval. That left the Justice Ministry handicapped. They told me they could only grant the written approval to visit Citibank. They expressed great displeasure with the change in position by Credit Suisse but said that now they too were concerned that something was wrong. They said that if I prepared a list of detailed questions, they would visit Credit Swiss and would get me the information. I was elated. They put one condition on however — that Mr. Gaussant, their Justice Department attorney, would have to be present when I questioned the Swiss bank officials.

It then occurred to me it would be a good idea to pay a courtesy call on our Ambassador to the U.S. mission in Geneva. I told the liaison that I would need some secretarial support on Saturday as we would be working, preparing for our Citibank meeting and the questions for Credit Suisse as well. Holy crap — you would have thought I had asked for the world to have a secretary come in and work on Saturday. After reminding them of the importance of the investigation and the authority we had, they found a secretary.

We had made the big breakthrough and since nothing could be set up until the next day, we had some of the weekend free. It was time to relax a little bit. George Kralis suggested that we go to the party held on occasional Fridays by the Marine detachment to the U.S. Mission. The party would be held at their villa overlooking Lake Geneva and was quite the gala. It gave an opportunity for U.S. personnel assigned to the embassy and other U.S. personnel to socialize without any foreign government staff present.

Of course, since Jim was armed, he would not be able to drink, relax, and enjoy himself. That's when George again came through. He volunteered to take us to the party and take care of security. Jim would check his revolver at the embassy and pick it up on our return. It was a terrific evening and wonderful opportunity to put the tensions of Iran-Contra behind and relax for a few hours.

The next morning it was back to the U.S. mission and I finished up the questions to give to attorney Gaussant to ask of Credit Suisse. Sunday again gave us a little opportunity to see some of the beauty of Switzerland. Jim and I rented a car and toured the Swiss Alps, visiting several delightfully scenic areas. We went up to the glacier where the James Bond movie "In his Majesty's Service" was filmed. We rode the cable car to the top for a great lunch, taking in the spectacular views along the way. We drove back to Geneva and had dinner at the restaurant in old town with the famous fondue. A little present for my unknowingly rising cholesterol levels.

Monday morning came quickly. With the bank records in hand and the questions ready to turn over to Gaussant, we headed for the train station. It was convenient for Gaussant, who lived in Bern. The train from Geneva to Zurich stopped at Bern. Gaussant was waiting, found the car we were in, boarded the train, and joined us for the rest of the trip. We were able to get an appointment with Gordon Insley at the Citibank office in Zurich.

He was practically at the front door waiting for us. He knew who Gaussant was and he was very well aware of who I was. Strangely enough, he asked Jim who he was and for his identification. When Jim produced his badge, Insely nervously announced to Jim, "I don't think you should be a part of these proceedings." Jim and I glanced at each other, I nodded to Jim it was alright and he excused himself to the adjacent room.

Gaussant and I sat down with Insley to begin our discussion.

Insley said he preferred to answer my questions personally but if there were some questions that he could not answer, he would bring in the knowledgeable bank personnel.

I placed the documents I had brought on Insley's desk and began to question him about it. His response to my first four or five questions were "That is too technical, I cannot answer that." At this point, I began to show obvious irritation. I told Insley I had 40 to 50 questions. Was he going to insist that I ask all 50 that he probably could not answer just so we could get to the right people? It would be a terrible waste of time.

After a bit of tense back and forth, he finally agreed. He brought in three other bank personnel, including a Mr. Christoffel. It turned out that Mr. Christoffel was the "unknown" bank employee who was since identified as making the wire transfer. One of the Vice Presidents of Citibank mistakenly had told New York that no such individual existed. That led us to believe that there had been a theft. Insley assured me that Christoffel was real and would vouch that he had in fact made the wire transfers to Credit Swiss.

At one point during the initial transfer however, Citibank in Zurich made an error. The Sultan of Brunei had asked for the money transfer to be encrypted or at least disguised. The bank planned to have the records show the money came from the Zurich branch rather than the Brunei branch. The Brunei branch then was to make a transfer in New York through the books of the Zurich branch.

Accidentally, a Citibank employee at the branch in Zurich misread a wire transfer message and ordered a second $10 million to be transferred. Another bank employee, Ann Jaggi, spotted the mistake and appropriately requested an investigation and reversal of the one entry. Otherwise, $20 million would have been on its way—$10 million compliments of the Sultan of Brunei and $10 million compliments of Citibank.

Both Christoffel and Jaggi produced evidentiary documents that I did not have. I asked them to make copies of them, implying that the copies I had were illegible. After going through all questions and the documentation, it was clear now that the money had left Citibank in Zurich and had been transferred to Credit Swiss in Geneva. At least now the trail was narrowing down. The documents even showed that Credit Swiss had "confirmed" the transfer out of Citibank's account at Credit Swiss to its ultimate destination which was to be the Enterprise account with the transposed Lake Resources number. It was evident that we could do no more at Citibank.

At that point, I reminded Insley that I was also representing the Sultan of Brunei. I asked Insley to call Mr. Possa at Credit Suisse Geneva to see if he could find out what happened to the Sultan's money. Insley flatly refused. At this point, Gaussant came to my rescue. He suggested that we get Possa on the phone so he could talk to him. I previously had provided Gaussant with the list of questions I had prepared the Saturday before. Earlier Gaussant had talked to Possa in connection with the release of the documents. The banker quickly connected the call and Gaussant started to question Possa.

Possa immediately became so obviously upset he asked Gaussant who was in the room with him. Gaussant advised that I was present and Possa insisted that Gaussant go to another room and call him for their discussion. Gaussant left and ten minutes later Gaussant reappeared with a strange smile on his face. He announced the mystery had been solved.

Apparently, as a result of my visit and the seriousness of the charges, Credit Suisse had begun examining of all of their records during that time period. They discovered they indeed had transferred the monies into the account that had the transposed number. In fact, that account was not active at the branch the money was sent to. However, the two final digits, which represent the branch and type of account were different since an account with that number had been in that branch but had been transferred to another branch. The manager just shipped the $10 million over to what he assumed was the proper branch and the money was placed in the account.

Shortly thereafter, the money was withdrawn by the surprised actual account owner and placed in a CD in another bank. Since that was a criminal violation of Swiss law, charges had been filed against the individual. Gaussant agreed to set up a meeting back in Geneva with the Swiss judge who was handling the case. I was delighted. My mission had been achieved. The missing money had been sort of located.

On my return to Geneva, I called Mark Belnick and told him that I had located the money. I gave him all the information I had at the time and told him I was meeting with the judge the next morning to see if I could find out a little more. I would try to determine the identity of the individual that received the money. That was the one last piece of the money puzzle Belnick needed.

The next morning back in Washington at the opening of the hearings, Senator Inouye proudly announced that I had found the money and would provide the rest of the details when I returned. I was excited as I assumed that meant that I would get my chance in the sun at the Iran-Contra hearings. Unfortunately, however, with all political grandstanding and the many other witnesses, that never materialized.

The next day Jim and I went over to the Justice Ministry in Geneva and I met with Judge Vladimir Stemberger. For a judge,

Stemberger seemed to be a little uptight. He appeared to be co-operative but at the same time a little reluctant to answer many of my questions. He confirmed what Gaussant had found out by telephone the day before. The money had passed into an individual's account who was not entitled to it. The individual took it from the bank and placed it in a certificate of deposit that was to mature in a few weeks. Stemberger advised that he had ordered the money frozen. He asked my thoughts on how the problem should be handled. I told him that since there was a gift involved, under U.S. laws the gift had not been consummated. The Sultan of Brunei wanted his money returned. In my view it should be done. Stemberger seemed to agree but said it would take some time to process the case and the transfer.

Then I asked the judge about the identity of the individual. Stemberger said he thought it would be inappropriate to bring this individual into our investigation since he was a prominent person in Swiss society. I pressed harder, asking him if the individual was in any way associated with any of the principles already under our investigation. I began naming the key names—Oliver North, Richard Secord, Albert Hakim, Willard Zucker, and so on. With each name I got a negative shake of the head. The best I could obtain from Stemberger, who was growing increasingly restless was a general description that the individual was about age 60, was a wealthy Swiss business person who had interests in shipping. He also mentioned the individual had a wife who was a doctor, and they were both prominent in Swiss society. That was apparently the main reason they were not going to release their names. God forbid their reputations be sullied by involvement in our investigation. I tried to keep pursuing the matter, but the judge only seemed to get more and more irritated with me. It was clear I was going to get nowhere, so I thanked him for the information and departed.

Too bad U.S. subpoenas don't work in Switzerland.

Upon my return to the U.S. mission to say my thank-yous and goodbyes, I was advised of Senator Inouye's opening statement at the Iran-Contra hearings that I had located the money. There was also a waiting call from Mark Belnick. Mark told me to be careful with the press in releasing any additional details before we had a chance to talk. My mission completed, I said goodbye to the ambassador. He invited me to a reception that evening at his home in honor of Barry Manilow who was replacing the recently deceased Red Skelton as a principal of UNICEF. A nice farewell to Switzerland.

Jim, George, and I had an opportunity to meet Barry Manilow but unfortunately, he did not do any entertaining. While chatting with various people at the reception, I was approached by a young woman who identified herself as Liza Schlein, a reporter with ABC news. I could not believe they had located me so quickly — and at the ambassador's residence no less! She began to question me about Senator Inouye's announcement about my locating the money. She no sooner got the question out when George spotted her talking to me. He recognized her and he and Jim rushed over and grabbed her and began to escort her out of the reception.

I said, "Hold it, it is our policy to cooperate with press. She told me who she was." Liza and I proceeded to have a cordial but very general conversation. I told her I could not release any details and that I was leaving in the morning. She asked if she could interview me at the airport. I told her she could, but she should be prepared to receive a "no comment" interview.

The next morning, we headed for the airport. We got there, and there was Liza and several TV cameras. Now things were getting exciting, I was back on television again. I answered some of her questions, sticking to the text of Senator Inouye's announcement and generally describing what I had done in Switzerland without providing any of the details. In a sense I felt a bit like a celebrity. It was kind of fun. All heads in the terminal were turned, wondering who the individual was that was being followed by the TV cameras. That said, I felt relieved to get on the plane. I ordered an airline martini and kicked back, my mission accomplished. Jim and I headed back to Washington. We arrived in Washington in the late afternoon. It wasn't too much of a surprise to see the media all lined up there as well. After all, they did have a pretty effective communications system. They had my flight number and were waiting.

Since Jim was the Chief of the Capitol Police Department, several police vehicles with uniformed officers were waiting at the off-ramp of the plane. Customs and immigration officials discreetly rushed us through their systems. However, as we entered the public area of the terminal, all of a sudden a huge panel of lights went on and a voice shouted out, "Mr. Cronin, can we speak to you for a moment?"

There were half a dozen representatives of the press and two or three TV cameras waiting in ambush. I gave them an additional "no comment" but while walking to the police cars waiting outside, I fielded a few general questions on my feelings on finding the money. I was riding high at this point. All heads turning, I again felt like a celebrity. Not bad for an Irish kid from New York. I was escorted into an awaiting police car and driven home. I had the records in my briefcase. Paying careful attention to the warnings of Belnick and having been out of town for 10 days, I suggested to the policemen that were taking me home that if there any members of the press on my private property I would appreciate them calling ahead and asking them to leave.

Lorraine was not aware of my exact arrival time at home. It

being a warm spring day, she was working around the house in shorts and bare feet—quite a sight as the police car pulled up. The two policemen proceeded to open the trunk of the car and hand me my briefcase. They also took out a shotgun from the trunk and proceeded to walk around the house and our two and a half acres in Great Falls—twice. They wanted to make sure there were no unwanted visitors. Lorraine didn't know what to think about the shotgun, and probably didn't want to know. The policemen were very friendly. They politely introduced themselves to her as I entered the house with my briefcase containing the newly found Swiss records. They told me to be very careful with the briefcase and keep it in a safe place. I chuckled at that as I put it under our bed.

It was a warm welcome returning to our office facility the next morning. As I entered, a number of people standing around looked at me and just began to applaud. That too made me feel like I had really accomplished something. Liman and Belnick thanked me for my efforts and we had a long meeting going over every step of the transactions. They told me to stand by to testify. But as I said, with the multitude of press, politicians, and other witnesses, I never got to testify live in front of the cameras at the hearings. That part of the investigation was personally disappointing.

Having found the Brunei money and completing the financial statements on the domestic fund-raising and the Enterprise, our work on the project was finally winding down. The hearings were about over and except for emergencies, such as some final clarification on the report to the Committee, we were beginning to return to a normal five-day workweek. The various Associate Counsels were responsible for preparing the final report material. We participated to a great degree in the chapters on the financial networks. Any counsel including financial data in the report had to run the draft through us to assure the financial data was prepared correctly.

22. Issues With The Central Intelligence Agency

In the course of our work, I felt the Iran-Contra investigation had revealed another opportunity. I observed that the Central Intelligence Agency was operating without much fiscal oversight. The House and Senate intelligence committees were somewhat small and understaffed. Even the Inspector General of the CIA was less than effective.

Early in the investigation, I had reviewed one of his reports. It was clear he had been lied to extensively but had made no attempt to press for the truth. Many of the disclosures I saw in the documents led me to conclude that parts of the CIA were pretty much out of control. They had massive slush funds and weapons stocks under the exclusive control of various CIA "proprietary" companies. Naturally, to disclose any of the details of these companies would injure our national security. As improper as some CIA operations may be, it still plays a very vital role in our national defense. The following episode describes activity that would get any agency *except* the CIA in all kinds of hot water—not just with Congress, but with U.S. law.

One of the undertakings of the Enterprise was the purchase of a ship called the Erria. We had documented the Erria's movements with the arms shipments and other activities which were set forth in detail in the committees' reports. One of the final entries in our report talks about a stranded weapons shipment onboard the Erria. It was about two million dollars worth of arms from an arms supplier in Portugal, a well known, world-wide illicit arms dealer. The name of the dealer was Defex. Even after the Iran-Contra blowup, the profiteering by the arms dealers continued. The weapons appeared on the open market at a cost of about two million dollars. Working through a series of intermediaries, the Enterprise turned up a buyer for the weapons. You guessed it, the Central Intelligence Agency turned out to be the buyer. They are also shrewd negotiators. They purchased weapons that were worth between two and 2.4 million dollars for $1.2 million, or about half of the value.

While these CIA transactions were disclosed in my report, I tried also to include other subsequent related events. Congress during this period of time had authorized both humanitarian and lethal aid for the Contras. The program was being operated by the CIA. The CIA turned around and bought the weapons (with Congress' money) from their own proprietary entities for more than twice what they paid for them. The difference between what Congress appropriated and what CIA actually paid was stashed away, hidden in several other of the CIA proprietaries. To me this was a clear attempt at pulling the wool over the taxpayers' and Congress' eyes — not to mention shorting the Contras.

I drafted up a section for the Report showing how this example was clear justification to take legislative action to authorize the General Accounting Office to do a full audit and investigation of the CIA. Arthur Liman sent me a note providing his full support for including the additional material in the Report. I discussed the issue with Senator Inouye, who also liked the idea. During one of our pre-hearing depositions with the House members, I had a chance to talk to Congressman Louis Stokes of Ohio, the Chairman of the House Intelligence Committee. We had a private one on one meeting. I told him about the transaction. He said if events actually happened that way, he would fully support the legislation to provide GAO authority to audit the CIA. During this time, I also had meetings with Comptroller General Bowsher and advised him of the results of my "lobbying" activities. He too believed the GAO should have the authority to look at CIA.

A few weeks before the issuance of the final report, I thought I would review the final draft to be sure the numbers were right. Much to my surprise, the recommendation for GAO to have authority to audit the CIA was missing. When I asked Liman and Belnick about the cleansing, all I got was a lot of stuttering and a very unclear explanation about how it was not directly part of the arms for hostages' deal.

Though that was technically correct, I felt it was still directly related. I could only assume that the CIA had used its muscle very effectively to have it erased completely out of the report. I guess they were more effective than my lobbying to get it in the report. I don't know what difference it would make. Instead, there was a recommendation to make the CIA Inspector General's line of reporting identical to that of the Inspector Generals of the other executive departments and agencies. Of course, to date even that has not happened. I doubt that with the strong lobbying power of the CIA, it will ever happen.

So, what is the final take-away of the Iran-Contra affair? The true and final conclusions will be set forth by historians. Unfortunately, the Reagan White House did not learn lessons from Watergate and history repeated itself. With regard to the question,

"Did the President know?" Only the former President of the United States, Ronald Reagan, can answer that question — and he is no longer with us.

The final report was issued and printed in the Congressional Record in November 1987. I returned to my more mundane projects at GAO. One memento hangs on my office wall today. It is a formal portrait of the entire Iran-Contra committee and all the staff. Ironically, when the picture was taken, the staff was moved around by the photographer. I was placed right under the American flag at the center of the group. Both Chairman Senator Inouye, and Senator Rudman, Vice Chairman, signed the picture which I will always cherish. Senator Inouye wrote, "To our chief accountant with the appreciation and admiration of Daniel Inouye." Senator Rudman wrote "With deep appreciation for all you did to unlock the secrets of Iran-Contra."

23. Was It Worth It?

I retired from the General Accounting Office in the summer of 1989. It was with a lump in my throat that I said goodbye to Chuck Bowsher, the Comptroller General, and my many other associates in GAO. It was hard to believe that 33 years of my life had gone by. However, I left with a sense of pride knowing I had served the U.S. taxpayers well. I had collected back from fraud and negligence hundreds of millions of dollars. I successfully developed improvements to the processes and policies of the financial management of the Government. Particularly satisfying were those recommendations that had to be implemented under "gunpoint" by the Congress.

During the last few years of my career as I would reminisce about various investigations, I began to hear the same comment over and over, "You ought to write a book." Well, here it is. I have written not just for the sake of reliving my career on these pages but for other, more important reasons.

From the time I became an Assistant Director in 1974, I had given numerous speeches to various governmental units, private organizations, state CPA societies, and colleges and universities. Several have been Keynote, addressing 500 to 1,000 people. The one I remember best however, was not a major speech. It was not a presentation to top government officials. It was a lecture on our auditing and investigating of the President of the United States which I gave at a local high school. My eldest son, then a senior at the school, asked me to speak to their college level government and history—Advanced Placement class, only available to seniors with high grade point averages. The course gave them college credits. This was not exactly a typical small high school classroom. Here I was in a lecture hall very similar to a college environment. I lectured on Watergate, subsequent investigations, on the various presidents, and the Iran Contra affair. The lecture lasted almost two hours. I left plenty of time for questions and dialogue with the students.

Most of the queries I had heard before and were easily answered, but a young lady raised her hand and asked one question that left me stumped momentarily.

"Mr. Cronin, considering all of the terrible things you told us about here this morning, and many other things I'm sure you have investigated and not told us about, don't you get concerned that our particular form of government is just not working?"

The room became hushed. I glanced at the two teachers who taught the course. The question had left them with their mouths open. All eyes were on me as the students waited for an answer. I gathered myself and thought for a moment and gave them my answer straight from the heart.

"No, actually it's just the opposite. It proves that our form of government really is working. After all, where else in the world, including many nations who are alleged to be free, can one individual do the things that I have done and made it home safely for dinner every night."

I concluded with a quote from Winston Churchill: "Democracy

is the worst form of government every invented by man, except for all the others."

Yes, the career was certainly worth it. From the $300 million I recovered for the taxpayers from the mortgage bankers in HUD insurance premiums, to Watergate, to Marcos, to Iran/Contra. Though I became known as "the Gatekeeper," I believe I closed my government career knowing that I had served my country well, both government and taxpayer.

The results and recommendations that came out of our financial audits and investigations seldom received front page coverage. When they did, with some notable exceptions, they quickly faded away from the public's interest. The most disconcerting thing about this is that today the scams and scandals of very similar natures keep recurring with only the names changed. It is my hope that this book will help guide the ever-changing leadership of our Government agencies and politicians to always be alert for fraud, waste, and abuse. If I may be so bold to say that I hope to have aided at least somewhat in reestablishing a long-needed improvement to our nation's moral compass.

The greatest frustration of it all, however, was that even at the end of my career, my counterparts in the corporate world and the private sector were making more than twice the amount of my federal salary. Fortunately for me, it was not just about the money. But I do fear that if in the future the government wants to recruit the best and the brightest, Congress must address the pay discrepancy.

Hopefully, some day that will happen, but if it does not, I urge those that have the qualifications to consider serving a term in Government. It is extremely rewarding, and you might make the Country even better than this investigator was able to do. I hope you have enjoyed reading this chronicle as much as I have enjoyed reliving my life with the General Accounting Office and the Congress of the United States.

About the Author

Cronin began his GAO career in 1956 and served in an ever-expanding watchdog capacity for thirty-three tumultuous years under six different Presidents. Reader beware, many of his investigations and assignments described herein necessarily had overlapping timelines. This book is a personal chronicle of his most notorious GAO investigations—directly as he witnessed them from the trenches. He led investigations and audits of Watergate, Marcosgate, Irangate, and many others—earning him the nickname "the Gatekeeper." His activities clearly dispense with the myth that accountants lead dull and boring lives.

CPSIA information can be obtained
at www.ICGtesting.com
Printed in the USA
BVHW082339120921
616612BV00004B/14